OVERLORD

D-Day and

the Invasion of Europe

Atheneum   1982   New York

OVERLORD
D-Day and the Invasion of Europe
ALBERT MARRIN

Picture Credits

National Archives: 5, 6-7, 12, 14, 19, 21, 25, 26, 28 (UPI), 52, 59,
69, 83, 89, 92-93, 99, 107, 114-115, 118-119, 127, 128-129,
142-143, 158-159, 163, 165
U.S. Air Force: 16-17, 40-41, 55, 122-123, 144-145, 166-167
U.S. Army: 35, 36, 38, 48, 72, 74, 135, 156
Public Archives Canada: 62 (#129059), 65 (#129056),
104 (#129053), 130 (#122765)
Imperial War Museum, London: 149, 168-169

Library of Congress Cataloging in Publication Data
Marrin, Albert.
Overlord: D-Day and the invasion of Europe.

Bibliography: p. 171
Includes index.
SUMMARY: Describes the events which occurred prior to,
during, and after the Allied invasion of Europe in 1944.
1. Operation Overlord—Juvenile literature.
2. World War, 1939-1945—Campaigns—France—Normandy—
Juvenile literature. 3. Normandy (France)—History—
Juvenile literature. [1. World War, 1939-1945—
Campaigns—France—Normandy. 2. Operation Overlord]
I. Title.
D756.5.N6M28   940.54'21   82-1745
ISBN 0-689-30931-7 ✓ AACR2

Published simultaneously in Canada by
McClelland & Stewart, Ltd.
Composition by American Book Graphic Services,
Brattleboro, Vermont
Printed and bound by Fairfield Graphics, Fairfield, Pennsylvania
Designed by Mary Ahern & Mina Greenstein
First Edition

This book is for Robert A. Kahn,
my friend

Contents

"You will enter the continent of Europe and . . .
undertake operations aimed at the heart of
Germany and the destruction of her armed
forces."

*Orders from the Allied Combined
Chiefs of Staff to
General Dwight D. Eisenhower
February 12, 1944.*

OVERLORD

D-Day and
the Invasion of Europe

1

Fortress Europe

It was a dull, breezy day at the Washington, D.C., airport. Storm clouds were gathering overhead as the big plane touched down on the runway. Its wheels screeched for a moment, then the pilot eased it to a stop near the long black car parked nearby. Propped against the car was a man wearing a floppy hat and metal-rimmed eyeglasses. Even at a distance his arms and shoulders seemed powerful. Steel braces encased his legs, which had been crippled for years by polio.

The plane's door opened. A stairway was rolled into place. And down came a short, balding man of sixty-seven. A big cigar was clasped in his teeth.

He marched over to the car, smiled a broad, friendly smile, and shook the hand of the waiting man. The car door slammed and Winston S. Churchill, prime minister of Great Britain, and Franklin D. Roosevelt, president of the United States, sped off toward the White House.

The world would never be the same again after their meeting.

Churchill and Roosevelt were friends, but it wasn't friendship that brought the Englishman across the Atlantic Ocean in the winter. The time was December 22, 1941, less than three weeks after the Japanese attack on Pearl Harbor. Churchill had come to Washington with his advisers for a special meeting. The aim of this meeting was to work out the main Allied plan for fighting World War II.

World War II was really *two* wars: against the Japanese Empire in Asia and against Adolf Hitler's Nazi Germany in Europe. What was the best way of fighting these wars? Should the Allies divide their power equally against each enemy? Or should they throw most of it against one enemy? If so, which one?

Japan, they knew, was a dangerous foe, but there was no chance of her forces reaching London, let alone Washington, D.C. Japan's warlords seemed satisfied to conquer the rich lands of Asia and the Pacific and use their natural resources for themselves.

But Germany was another matter. Adolf Hitler, the man Germans called *Der Fuehrer* — The Leader —

Master of all he surveys. German dictator Adolf Hitler poses with the Eiffel Tower in the background during a visit to Paris, spring 1940.

dreamed of ruling the world. Hitler believed that most of the world's peoples were racially inferior to the Ger-

With the Arch of Triumph in the background, German troops parade down one of Paris's main avenues after the city's surrender.

mans. His people, he said, were "Aryans" — blond, blue-eyed "supermen" who had the right to conquer and enslave others. Certain people, like the Jews, who Hitler believed were totally evil, would be killed to the last man, woman, and child. Hitler's dreams were crazy, yet Roosevelt and Churchill feared they might come true. And so

they decided to fight the Japanese with the smallest forces they could, while doing everything possible to defeat Germany. Once Germany was defeated, they'd concentrate their whole might on the Japanese.

They made a wise choice; for to help his dreams come true, Hitler had built the most powerful war machine the world had ever seen. Millions of highly trained warriors — soldiers, sailors, airmen — obeyed his commands. Already they had crushed one great nation after another. Poland, Norway, Holland, Belgium, and France had fallen in a few days or weeks. Denmark was taken over in a single day. By December, 1941, *Der Fuehrer* was master of Western Europe. His planes were bombing Britain and his tanks stood at the gates of Moscow, the Russian capital. His favorite soldier, Field Marshal Erwin Rommel, the "Desert Fox," was racing with his army across North Africa toward the Suez Canal in Egypt. If he captured the Suez Canal, the British would be unable to send men and supplies to their possessions in Asia. Nothing would be able to save these colonies from capture by the Japanese. It was a horrible time, that December of 1941.

Yet slowly, painfully, things began to improve during the next two years. There were many reasons for this improvement, but together they meant that the Allies were evening the odds. The Germans, confident that whatever they did would succeed, began to get careless. They made mistakes, which the Allies quickly turned to their advantage. For instance, instead of building heavy long-range bombers to destroy the British aircraft industry, they attacked with light, medium-range bombers. The result was that the RAF — Royal Air Force — drove the *Luftwaffe* — German air force — from Great Britain's skies.

The Allies also had the advantage when it came to spies. One of their spies had stolen plans for the machine the Germans used for putting their secret radio messages into code. "Ultra," as the machine was called, allowed the Allies to read every radio message the Germans sent during the war. There were times when the Allied high command knew Hitler's plans before his orders reached his generals in the field. Having Ultra was as if the Allies had hundreds of thousands of extra fighting men and weapons.

Finally, there was the Allied fighting man himself. The American, British, and Russian soldier proved to be every bit as brave and tough as Hitler's "supermen." Besides, once the Allies' war efforts got into full swing, they were able to outnumber and outproduce the Germans by better than two to one. The result was that by the end of 1942, the Russians had stopped the German advance and began to push them back; the Americans and British had chased Rommel out of North Africa. By the end of 1943, they had crossed the Mediterranean Sea from North Africa to invade Italy. Soon they had knocked Hitler's ally, Benito Mussolini, the Italian dictator, out of the war.

Yet the Allied leaders were not satisfied. At the rate things were going, they knew it would take many years to defeat Germany. From Russia to North Africa to Italy, Hitler's generals had made the Allies buy each victory at a terrific price in soldiers' and civilians' lives. The Russians alone lost over two million killed in 1943, plus thousands of villages and towns burned to the ground.

There was only one way to end the war quickly, thereby saving millions of other lives. Using England as a base, British and American armies would have to cross the English Channel, land in Nazi-occupied France, and stab into the heart of Germany.

Planning for this invasion began early in 1942. Like everything the military does that must be kept secret, the invasion plan was given a code name. OVERLORD. It stood for the whole Allied plan to invade Europe and win the war.

Before OVERLORD was finished, hundreds of other secret plans would have to become part of it. Each of these plans also had a code name. Next to OVER-LORD itself, Operation NEPTUNE was the most important. Neptune was the ancient Roman god of the sea, and this plan had to do with his kingdom: it was the one to transport the Allied armies across the English Channel and land them on the shores of France.

And NEPTUNE would begin on D-Day. Every time soldiers plan an operation for some unknown date in the future, that day is called "D-Day." There were many D-Days during World War II, but none was as important as this one.

Der Fuehrer and his generals didn't know when or where, but they knew that sooner or later *the* D-Day would come and they'd have to fight off an invasion by the Allied powers. There was no choice for them. Either they repelled the invasion or lost the war. And if they lost the war, they would probably lose their lives, because they would be put on trial as war criminals and hanged if found guilty. For them, it was victory or death.

In 1942, Hitler ordered work to begin on the "Atlantic Wall." This was not to be a high, solid wall like the Great Wall of China. Instead, Hitler wanted as many as fifteen thousand steel and concrete forts built along the seacoast from Norway to Spain. These forts would cover every possible landing place for twenty-five hundred miles and be able to destroy the Allies the moment they landed.

Thousands of slave laborers worked day and night to build the Atlantic Wall. They poured millions of tons of concrete, so much that it became scarce throughout Nazi-occupied Europe. Steel also became so scarce that old railroad track and other scrap metal had to be torn up and reused.

Each fort had walls six feet thick and was dug fifty or more feet into the ground. Its top was disguised as a house, barn, or church complete with a steeple and a cross. But it packed a terrific punch, usually a battery of long-range coastal defense guns. These guns could easily throw a thousand-pound high-explosive shell five miles out to sea.

Hitler's forts had all the comforts of home — and more. There, four stories beneath the ground, soldiers lived in barracks with central heating, electric light, air-conditioning, radios, telephones, workshops, and large supplies of food and ammunition. One fort even had a fancy underground bar for officers, complete with over-stuffed chairs and wood-paneled walls.

Yet there were German officers who had little faith

in the Atlantic Wall. There was much work still to do before it was finished. But even then they felt that it wouldn't be able to hold off the Allies.

Field Marshal Gerd von Rundstedt, commander-in-chief of Germany's armies in the West, was one of these doubters. At sixty-nine, Rundstedt was the only German field marshal who had never lost a battle. It was he who had masterminded the earlier victories in Poland, France, and Russia.

Rundstedt was a good soldier, but he had no respect for his *Fuehrer,* calling him "that corporal, Hitler." He had even less respect for the Atlantic Wall, which he told everyone was an "enormous bluff."

Rundstedt believed that the Germans were only fooling themselves if they thought the Atlantic Wall could keep out the Allies. They could break through at any point between Norway and Spain; but he believed they were most likely to attack across the English Channel to France. That's what *he* would do in their place. France was the logical place to invade, because it was close to England's major ports and within easy reach of Allied air power. Of course the Americans and British would pay heavily for a breakthrough, but no amount of steel and concrete could keep them off the French beaches if that was where they wanted to go.

"All right, then," Rundstedt thought, "let them

The face of the enemy. Field Marshal Gerd von Rundstedt didn't look like a very friendly fellow. He was commander of all the German armies in the West.

land." He would keep his panzer divisions behind the coast, out of range of Allied naval guns. *"Panzer"* is German for "armor"; a panzer division was an armored, or tank, division. When the enemy landed, he would let them pack their troops and supplies into the narrow beaches. Then he'd send in the panzer divisions, backed by every man, gun, and plane he could get, to smash the Allies and throw them back into the sea.

Erwin Rommel didn't believe this plan would work either. After being outfoxed in North Africa, in January 1941, the Desert Fox was put in charge of defenses along the English Channel. Although under Rundstedt's command, Rommel, as Hitler's favorite, could go straight to *Der Fuehrer* whenever they disagreed. And they disagreed often. Rundstedt couldn't get along with the younger man. He called the fifty-two-year-old Rommel *"Marschall Bubi"* — "Marshall Little Guy."

Rommel had learned the hard way that air power made the difference between victory and defeat. You could have the best soldiers in the world, but they would be dead ducks unless protected by an umbrella of airplanes. By the beginning of 1944, the *Luftwaffe* could no longer be counted on to give that protection. Massing forces behind the coast as Rundstedt wanted would make them easy targets for the Allied air forces, which were becoming more powerful every day.

Although von Rundstedt was his superior, Field Marshal Erwin Rommel was Hitler's favorite officer and commander of the German defenses along the coast of occupied France.

A close-up view of a German work party on a Normandy beach. This picture, showing the men running for cover, was made by low-flying U.S. fighter plane. The picture shows wooden ramps and posts tipped with Teller mines.

Rommel believed that the first hours of D-Day would decide who won or lost the war. Once the Allies came ashore and dug in, they could never be driven back into the sea. Germany's defenses, then, should be set up to stop the enemy at the water's edge. "The war will be won or lost on the beaches," Rommel told an aide. "The high-water line must be the main fighting line."

Rundstedt's master plan still held, but Rommel was allowed to go ahead with his ideas also. On his orders the shore defenses of the Atlantic Wall were strengthened until they became the strongest on earth.

From the port city of Calais in the north to Cherbourg in the south, he created a "Zone of Death" along the English Channel. The zone began six to seven miles behind the beaches, where dikes were opened and rivers blocked to create vast flooded areas and swamps. These would cut off the beaches from the mainland and drown any paratroopers dropped behind the lines.

Rommel was worried about Allied paratrooper and glider forces. Possible landing places that couldn't be flooded were filled with "Rommel's asparagus." These were four-foot high wooden posts driven into the ground and linked with trip wires attached to cannon shells. A glider coming in for a landing would either crack-up on the posts or be blown to bits when it hit the wires and set off the shells.

Rommel placed mines everywhere: in the fields, in the gullies leading from the beaches, in the sand dunes, and in the beaches themselves. His mines were usually of two types. The Teller mine was set to explode whenever anything weighing 250 pounds or more went over it, such as a tank or truck. The S-mine was more delicate. A man only had to touch a trip wire and the mine would explode into hundreds of small steel balls. Rommel had nearly six million mines planted in the months before D-Day. Signs with a black skull and crossbones and the words

The Germans were masters of camouflage. Here a concrete fort is disguised to look like an ordinary wood-timbered French house. This particular fort contained an observation post and a powerful coastal defense cannon.

"*Achtung, Minen*" — "Attention, Mines" — warned people to keep their distance.

In addition to the giant forts, Rommel had all kinds of smaller strongpoints built on the cliffs overlooking the coastline. Mortars and powerful eighty-eight-millimeter cannon were roofed with concrete. Concrete pillboxes with twin machine guns were set into the cliffs themselves. Every weapon was placed to create a deadly crossfire or to shoot straight down the beach, knocking down the invaders in rows as they came out of their landing boats.

The defenses became thicker along the beaches. Machine gun nests, covered slit trenches, and barbed wire entanglements were built. Rommel also had several secret weapons. In some places he had automatic flamethrowers fed from underground pipelines that ran to gasoline tanks hidden behind the beaches. All that a Nazi soldier had to do was see the enemy coming from his post atop the cliff, flick a switch, and then watch part of the beach turn into an ocean of flames.

Not satisfied with securing the beaches, Rommel pushed his defense line into the sea. "Hedgehogs" lay in rows underwater along stretches of beach near towns or roads leading inland. These looked like the jacks children

Hitler and his lieutenants examine an unmanned miniature tank. Such devices were packed with explosives and were intended to be sent toward the Allied lines and detonated by remote control. In spite of the high hopes placed on them, they were a total failure when the real invasion came.

play with, but were made of seven-foot lengths of steel riveted together to tear out the bottom of a landing boat. "Dragon teeth," sharp concrete pyramids six feet high and weighing a ton, waited for enemy tanks. Wooden ramps and heavy stakes were mined; the ramps not only exploded, but were built to expose the thin undersides of tanks to gunfire from the shore.

Finally, there were the Belgian Gates, which the Allies called "Element C." Imagine the heaviest iron fence you have ever seen. That's what one of these barriers was like. Each weighed three thousand pounds and was nine feet high and nine feet wide. Separate sections, each mined, were joined together to form a long fence to keep landing craft away from the beaches.

The Germans were beginning to feel pretty good by the spring of 1944. Anyone who visited the coast under Rommel's command saw layer after layer of defenses. He had kept his promise to turn the coast of France into a zone of death. Radio Berlin was so proud of what he had done that it challenged the Allies: "Come on, if you dare."

That is exactly what they were preparing to do.

2

Buildup

In January, 1944, at the same moment Rommel began his job in France, the third son of a Kansas dairy farmer arrived in England. Born in 1890, a year before Rommel, this man was well-liked by all who knew him. He had a wonderful smile and an easy-going manner. "He looks sort of like the guys at home," said one United States Army private. His name was General Dwight David Eisenhower, or "Ike" for short.

Ike had come to England to take up a new job. His title was Supreme Commander, Allied Expeditionary Forces, Europe. In other words, this man from Kansas was lord of OVERLORD. If it succeeded, he would get the credit. If it failed, he, and he alone, would be blamed.

Eisenhower had never led an army in battle. His real abilities were in planning and in helping others work together. These were the skills that made him the perfect choice for supreme commander.

As soon as he arrived in England, Eisenhower chose his assistant commanders. It didn't make any difference to him if these were Americans or Englishmen, so long as they were the best people for the job.

Englishmen did in fact get many of the top OVER-LORD posts. They had plenty of experience fighting Nazi Germany, and the invasion would be launched from their country. The post of deputy supreme commander went to Air Chief Marshal Sir Arthur Tedder, who had commanded the air forces fighting Rommel in North Africa. The Allied naval commander was Admiral Sir Bertram H. Ramsay, a veteran of forty years in the Royal Navy. Air Chief Marshal Sir Trafford Leigh-Mallory, the Allied air commander, was a famous fighter pilot.

These men were OVERLORD's chief planners, but they would not lead its armies into battle on D-Day. The American forces would be led by General Omar N. Bradley. "Brad," as his friends called him, was a thoughtful, soft-spoken man who looked like a schoolteacher. He was also an experienced soldier, who had commanded American troops in North Africa and Sicily. Now Ike had given him the most important assignment of his life.

The lord of OVERLORD. General Dwight D. Eisenhower, Supreme Commander, Allied Expeditionary Forces in Europe. His genial smile and politeness played a critical part in getting the Allied leaders to work together in harmony.

The British battle commander was Field Marshal Sir Bernard Law Montgomery, one of the finest soldiers his country has ever had. "Monty" knew war from the foot soldier's mud-eye view. As a platoon leader in World War I, he had been so seriously wounded that he had nearly died. Although Monty became a field marshal, his soldiers still loved him. They knew that he loved them and that their lives were precious to him. He would never begin a battle without first making sure that things were, as he said, "all tickety-boo" — perfect. Monty would rather lose a thousand guns than one gunner.

Ike and his officers had to plan the largest military operation in history. But before they could think of anything else, they had to decide *where* to strike. They couldn't simply pick any spot along the coast from Norway to Spain and put an army ashore there. They needed an area that had long stretches of hard-packed beach for unloading troops and supplies. This area also had to be near a major seaport that could be captured quickly, otherwise reinforcements couldn't be brought in fast enough. Finally, the area had to be within fighter plane range of bases in England in order to protect the beachheads.

The best place for an invasion was an area known as the Pas de Calais. This area is on a stretch of French

Air Chief Marshal Sir Trafford Leigh-Mallory, the Allied Air Commander for OVERLORD, was a famous fighter pilot. He was killed in an airplane crash toward the end of the war.

coast that is less than twenty-one miles from England; on a clear day you can see the white cliffs of Dover across the water. The problem with the Pas de Calais was that the Germans also thought it the best site for an invasion. Rommel had put his strongest defenses there. He would have liked nothing better than for Eisenhower to be foolish enough to land in that area.

The next best landing place is five times the distance from England as the Pas de Calais. This is a beautiful area of dairy farms, apple orchards, and seaside vacation spots. It is called Normandy.

If you hold your left thumb and forefinger like a cocked pistol, you'll have a pretty good idea of what the Normandy coast looks like. The thumb would be the Contentin Peninsula jutting out into the English Channel; the great port of Cherbourg is at its tip. Moving northward, the area from the base of the thumb to the end of the forefinger would be the Normandy invasion beaches.

These beaches stretched for fifty miles from the base of the Contentin Peninsula to the mouth of the Orne River. Eight miles upstream from here is the city of Caen, where most of Normandy's important roads and railway lines meet. Rommel wanted to defend the coast of Normandy as heavily as the Pas de Calais. Luckily for the Allies, he hadn't finished the job by the time they were ready to begin OVERLORD.

Field Marshal Bernard Montgomery. An experienced battlefield commander, ''Monty,'' as he was affectionately called, always moved cautiously to avoid unnecessary casualties.

The Allies planned to have one hundred seventy-five thousand troops ashore in Normandy by D-Day evening. Their forces were to land along five sections of the coast, each section having its own code name. Two sections were assigned to the United States First Army under General Bradley. The first section was called Utah Beach, and it stretched for some five miles along the base of the Contentin Peninsula. The second section was Omaha Beach, twelve miles southeast of Utah.

The rest of the coast was assigned to the British Second Army under Field Marshal Montgomery. Gold, Juno, and Sword Beach stretched eastward from Omaha to the mouth of the Orne River. Gold and Sword were to be taken by British divisions, Juno by the Canadians.

Eisenhower gathered his forces for the coming battle. American soldiers poured into England during 1943 and the first half of 1944. Most of these crossed the Atlantic in convoys of dozens of troop ships guarded by long-range airplanes and submarine-killing destroyers. The Allies had lost millions of tons of shipping to Nazi submarines at the beginning of the war and weren't taking any unnecessary chances now.

Some Americans came over on fast British ocean liners like the *Queen Mary* and *Queen Elizabeth,* which could outrun any submarine. These ships were crowded, holding as many as fifteen thousand men each. The soldiers were cramped belowdecks into bunks stacked four-high. The food was awful, but this made no difference to most of the men, who were too seasick to eat. Of the million-and-a-half servicemen brought across the Atlantic before D-Day, not one was lost to enemy action at sea.

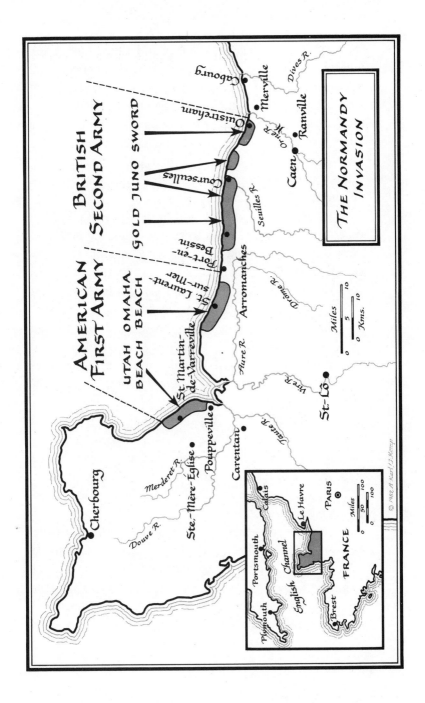

THE NORMANDY INVASION

BRITISH SECOND ARMY

GOLD JUNO SWORD

AMERICAN FIRST ARMY

UTAH OMAHA BEACH BEACH

Cherbourg

Ste.-Mère Eglise

Pouppeville

Carentan

St.Martin-de-Varreville

St. Laurent-sur-Mer

Arromanches

Port-en-Bessin

Courseulles

Ouistreham

Cabourg

Merville

Ranville

Caen

St.-Lô

Douve R.

Merderet R.

Taute R.

Aure R.

Vire R.

Drôme R.

Seulles R.

Orne R.

Dives R.

Miles
0   5   10
0 Kms.   10

Cherbourg

Plymouth

Portsmouth

Le Havre

Calais

PARIS

FRANCE

Brest

English Channel

Miles
0   50   100
0   100

© 1982 A Karl/J Kemp

Their landing began what is still called "the Yank invasion of England." English people and Americans did not get used to each other easily. So much about them was different, including their language. Although they used the same words, these didn't always mean the same thing. It took the GIs (GI stands for "Government Issue") a while to get used to the fact that a "lift" was an elevator, "petrol" was gasoline, and the "underground" was the subway.

The English never got used to the colorful GI slang. When a soldier asked a girl to go "sidewalk slapping," he wanted to go for a walk. "Grab a wing" meant "Hold my hand." "Let's cut a rug" was only an invitation to dance, not to wreck the house. And "Do you dig me?" was just another way of saying "Do you understand me?"

Food was a more serious problem. Great Britain was too small a country to supply its own food needs *and* those of over a million GIs. Food was rationed, and anyone who wasted even a small scrap was made to feel unpatriotic.

The GIs hated the British wartime diet. It was said that Brussels sprouts were served with each meal, including breakfast. Dried milk, powdered eggs, and boiled kidneys were also served regularly. The GIs thought British sausages were filled with sawdust, calling them "sawdust in battledress."

Thousands of tons of food had to be shipped from the United States. This meant giving valuable cargo space to items like frankfurters and peanut butter instead of bombs and spare parts. But the high command thought the sacrifice had to be made. As one GI said, "I think the first shipment of peanut butter saved our lives."

United States Army bases became little corners of home in the English countryside. English visitors couldn't believe their eyes when they saw the piles of hot dogs and hamburgers, and how they were washed down with a strange drink called "Coke."

The GIs were generous, especially to the English children. They took up collections for orphans and the sick. Wherever American troops were stationed, it was Christmas all year long, with thousands of Santa Clauses. When a GI was invited to an English home, he brought food. And such food! Items like *pails* of GI ice cream. Airmen liked to mix sweet cream and cutup peaches, cherries, and other fruit in 20-gallon cans. They'd put a can in a bomber and come back from a trip at 25,000 feet with the mixture frozen just right.

There were many black GIs in England. The people had never seen so many black men at once and in the same place. They were fascinated by these strangers from across the sea. Many were farm boys from the deep South, who spoke with a slow, easy drawl. Others were gum-chewing, fast-talking city slickers from places like Harlem and Detroit. Hundreds of black troops would be marching as a sergeant called the cadence: "Hut, two, three, four." All of a sudden the men would take up the rhythm and break into a jitterbug step. Many of the black soldiers came from poor families back home. They understood what it meant to be hungry and do without the necessities of life. And no one was more generous to the needy than they.

Yet manpower alone can't win wars. Warriors need the tools of war, and these can only come from factories on the "home front." In England, the government drafted women to work in the war factories, just as it drafted most of the men for the armed forces. The English produced enormous amounts of war materials, but nothing compared to what the Americans were doing. The United States is a very much larger country, and it wasn't necessary to draft nearly every healthy man for the services. They could stay at home and work.

And work they did! By 1944, nearly eighteen million Americans, men and women, were doing war work. They poured out a stream of war materials to the fighting fronts. By May, 1944, they had sent over five-and-a-half million tons of supplies across the Atlantic for D-Day.

So much material arrived that small railroads had to be built to remove it from the docks to storage areas. These areas held three hundred twenty thousand different items ranging from millions of dental fillings and brooms to complete field hospitals.

England became a giant warehouse for American military hardware. Any youngster out for a bicycle ride along a quiet country lane might pass ammunition dumps lining both sides of the road, hidden under sheets of artificial grass. Thousand-pound bombs were piled in rows one on top of the other; you could walk on them, even throw rocks at them, and they wouldn't go off as long as their fuses weren't screwed into place. Tons of cannon shells were kept in roadside bins. The United States Army stockpiled more ammunition in England for D-Day than had been fired in all of World War I.

But it was the machines that were really amazing. Fighter planes were parked in fields in lines, one next to

A few of the light trucks gathered for OVERLORD parked in a muddy English field.

the other, as far as the eye could see. Each plane's motor was still covered with the waterproof canvas it had been wrapped in for its trip across the ocean; its tail had still not been attached to the fuselage. Each plane waited for the mechanics to assemble it for battle.

Tanks, armored cars, jeeps, bulldozers, trucks, ambulances, and ten-ton wreckers were lined up by the thousands in fields and along roadsides.

American fighters waiting to be made battle-ready.
The planes in this row are P-47 Thunderbolts, the other
are P-51 Mustangs.

Certain valleys held the most amazing sight of all:
railway equipment. Ike's planners expected to use the
French railways once their armies had a beachhead. To
replace destroyed equipment, they stockpiled twenty
thousand freight cars and one thousand new locomotives.

England seemed to be growing in front of its people's

eyes. They stared at the war supplies piled on their tiny island, wondering if it would be able to hold them all. They joked about how only the steel anchor wires of the antiaircraft barrage balloons floating overhead kept Britain from sinking into the sea. These balloons were giant, sausage-shaped bags filled with helium gas and were used to keep low-flying enemy planes away from a target.

It was one thing to gather soldiers and supplies in Britain, another to carry them safely across the English Channel to Normandy. To do this OVERLORD's planners needed special kinds of boats for landing troops and supplies on shore; that is why the serial numbers painted on their sides always began with the letter L — for "landing."

Some of these were built to carry only soldiers. The LCA, or Landing Craft Assault, was a small boat carried aboard a mother ship; when lowered into the water, it could bring thirty men to shore. The LCI, or Landing Craft Infantry, traveled on the sea by itself. It was 158 feet long and could bring 200 soldiers onto a beach.

Other ships delivered fighting machines. The LCTs, or Landing Craft Tanks, ferried tanks and cannon ashore. But the LSTs, Landing Ship Tanks, were the workhorses of any invasion fleet. The British had invented the LST by cutting the bow off a tanker and fitting it with double doors and a ramp. The lower deck of an LST was crowded with tanks; the upper deck had trucks and jeeps lined up bumper to bumper. As soon as the assault troops won a beachhead, the LSTs would ground themselves as close as possible to the beach at low tide. The tanks would roll out quickly, their guns loaded and ready for action.

Saddling up. LSTs, their jaws open and ramps down are loading men and vehicles at a seaport somewhere in England.

Then elevators would bring the vehicles from above to the lower deck and they too would land. The grounded LST had to wait only a few hours for the incoming high tide to refloat it.

The strangest invasion craft of all was neither a boat nor a truck, but both rolled into one. The DUKW, a truck with the hull of a boat, looked like something out of a Walt Disney comic strip. The "Donald Duck," as it was nicknamed, could cut through the water like a boat. When it reached solid ground, it waddled ashore and moved ahead on wheels. There was nothing like a "duck" for getting out of the water and over a beach quickly to safety from enemy gunfire.

Although special boats could land a force to seize a beachhead, they couldn't bring in supplies for the large army OVERLORD needed for the great battles to come. "Logistics" is the science of supplying armies in battle. It is one of the rules of logistics that eight tons of supplies must come ashore with each fighting man, then one ton a month just to keep him going. A single division — fourteen thousand men — needed one hundred twelve thousand tons of supplies when it landed and at least 466 tons a day as long as it remained in battle.

Ike knew that Cherbourg couldn't be captured for a while after D-Day. Even then the enemy was sure to wreck its port before the Allies marched in. OVER-LORD'S planners decided that the only thing to do was to bring along a few seaports with them.

There were some strange ideas about how to do this. The British had a plan to freeze salt water mixed with chunks of wood into huge floating piers that carried their own workshops, antiaircraft guns, and refrigerating plants to keep them from melting. Some "Habakkuks," as they were called, would be so large that they could be used as floating airfields.

This idea was finally dropped in favor of MUL-BERRY, the code name for the two harbors that were to be built in England and floated across the Channel. MULBERRY A would be anchored off the American beaches, MULBERRY B off the British beaches.

Old American merchant ships were deliberately sunk off the Normandy beaches to form breakwaters so that the supply convoys unloading offshore would not be bounced around as much by the rough seas.

Building two artificial harbors is not as simple as it sounds. The weather in the English Channel is usually stormy and the water rough. A harbor must be sheltered, because you can't unload a ship when it is being smashed by six-foot waves.

To calm the water around the harbor, old ships would be filled with cement and sunk in line to form an outer breakwater off the Normandy beach. Then hundreds of hollow concrete blocks, each the size of a five-floor apartment house laid on its side, would be floated into place and sunk, forming an inner breakwater.

Each of these blocks would have antiaircraft guns and living quarters for those who manned them. Finally, ships would pull up to long floating piers and unload their cargos into trucks, which would drive to shore over floating roadways. The piers and roadways were built to move up and down with the tide.

Bringing in oil and gasoline was another problem. Tankers were easy targets for enemy planes. PLUTO was the answer to the fuel problem. The letters stood for (P)ipe (L)ine (U)nder (T)he (O)cean. Hundreds of miles of plastic pipe were made in Britain. The plan was for ships to lay the pipe across the floor of the English Channel. The ends would then be connected to pumping stations in Britain and to storage tanks in France.

Some of this fuel would keep the "Funnies" in action; they were called "Funnies" because they looked like creatures from a zoo on another planet. They were really tanks invented by the British to do special jobs. No one laughed when they went into battle.

Engineers fitted thirty-ton Sherman and Churchill tanks with "bloomers." These bloomers were canvas collars that surrounded the tank and could be inflated like a giant life preserver to keep it afloat. Each tank was also waterproofed and had rear propellers like a boat. When lowered into the sea from a ship, it was supposed to swim to shore with the first waves of infantry landing craft.

Need to clear a path through a mine field? Then the "Crab" is what you want. Each "Crab" tank had heavy chains attached to a steel spool mounted in front. When the tank came to a mine field, the spool began to whirl the chains, slapping them against the ground. The mines were set off, clearing the way for the infantry.

Maybe you've got to cross a ditch or a rushing stream? Send for an "Ark," an Armored Ramp Carrier. This tank carried two steel runways that could be raised or lowered as needed.

Is an enemy pillbox slowing up things with its machine guns? Call a "Crocodile," the most unfunny of the Funnies. The Crocodile's cannon did not fire normal shells. Instead it squirted streams of flaming napalm a distance of 360 feet. Napalm is gasoline that has been turned into a jelly; it burns at a temperature of one thousand degrees and sticks to anything it touches like chewing gum.

Victory or defeat for OVERLORD depended not only on having more men and machines than the enemy, but on having more information than he did. This information had to be gathered bit by bit, often in dangerous ways.

OVERLORD'S planners had to learn everything they could about the geography of Normandy. In May, 1942, the British Admiralty asked anyone who had traveled in France before the war to send in whatever snapshots and picture postcards they had. Nine million pictures were received, and five hundred thousand of these were copied for the Admiralty's photographic library.

These pictures showed things that could not be learned in any other way. A narrow path led up behind a cliff where Rommel had put some heavy guns. Or a back alley ran behind a beachside hotel the enemy was using as an observation post.

Pilots buzzed the beaches at ground level with high-speed cameras. Every inch of the defenses was photographed and the pictures put together to form a gigantic photomap of Normandy. Every house, every gun position, and every tank trap was noted on the map. On D-Day each Allied warship knew what targets it had to hit and where they were.

Scientists studied books and charts 200 and 300 years old to learn about the tides off the Normandy beaches. Frogmen swam ashore at night, hiding from German patrols that passed near them in the darkness. They were armed, not with guns, but with maps and surveyor's tools. They measured distances, checked sandbars, and drew diagrams of pathways leading inland from the beaches.

General Bradley once said he wasn't sure if the sand at a certain spot on Omaha Beach was packed hard enough to support tanks. Next morning British frogmen came to a meeting with sand samples. They had landed in Normandy a few hours before and returned with proof that the spot could support tanks.

It is one thing to learn the enemy's secrets, another to keep him from learning your own. There was plenty the Germans could learn about OVERLORD. As the planners went about their work, they created mountains of paper. For example, 800 typed pages were needed for a *short* summary of the naval plan; a complete set of the actual naval orders, plus maps, weighed over 300 pounds. The completed D-Day plan for General Bradley's First Army was bound in a mimeographed book with more words than some encyclopedias. The Air Force plans were so large that it was said the invasion would begin when the paper work equaled the weight of the planes. Yet losing just one sheet of paper might have tipped off the enemy to the whole plan.

To make sure that this didn't happen, OVERLORD was protected by CIC — Counter Intelligence Corps — made up of hundreds of specially trained agents. CIC poked its nose into everything. At headquarters, its men even went around at night pulling file cabinet and desk drawers to make sure they were locked.

They were especially interested in going through office waste baskets. For a colonel might receive a note with some secret information and throw it away when he finished reading it instead of destroying it. All waste paper at planning headquarters was treated as "Top Secret." Field Marshal Montgomery used to tell of a chaplain at headquarters who marked his files "Sacred" and "Top Sacred."

CIC agents spied on everyone who knew anything about OVERLORD. One person "in the know" couldn't keep his mouth shut. He was a United States Air Force major general who had been Ike's classmate at West Point. He got drunk one night at a party and bragged about how much he knew. The quiet English waiter happened to be an agent and reported what he overheard. A few hours later Ike knew the story and the major general was on a ship bound for home, his military career ruined. He had been broken to a colonel's rank and would spend the rest of the war at a lonely base in the Midwest. With Ike, there was no such thing as "letting it slide," even for an old friend, when his men's lives were at stake.

Even so, there were some close calls with OVER-LORD secrets. On a warm day in May, 1944, workers in a room in the British War Office in London opened a window to get some fresh air. On a nearby desk lay twelve copies of a top-secret set of D-Day papers. Suddenly a gust of wind picked up the papers and scattered them like confetti on the street below.

Soldiers raced down the stairs and into the street. After a two-hour search they recovered eleven copies; copy number twelve was nowhere to be found. "Where is it?" they wondered. Worse "Who *has* it?"

Their questions were answered later that day when a British soldier who had been standing guard duty across the street returned the missing copy. A stranger had handed it to him. To this day no one knows who that stranger was, except that the soldier said he wore thick eyeglasses and probably had poor vision. OVERLORD was safe, but from then on the windows in the office were nailed shut, and kept shut no matter how warm it became indoors.

OVERLORD's secrets remained safe; safe, that is, except for the fact that the Allies were planning an invasion. This fact could not be hidden. The Germans knew that American men and supplies were pouring into Britain.

They also read American and British newspapers, and these always spoke of the invasion that would begin someday.

Someday! But *what* day? And *where?* These were the two great secrets of OVERLORD. If the enemy found the answers to these questions, the Allies would be beaten before they started.

Winston Churchill once said that, in war, truth is so precious that it must be protected by "a bodyguard of lies." What Churchill meant was that you must bluff the enemy, making him lower his guard at the place you plan to attack.

OVERLORD was surrounded by such a bodyguard of lies. The aim of these lies was to make the Germans believe two things. First, to convince them *before* D-Day that the invasion would come in the Pas de Calais. Second, to convince them *after* D-Day that the Normandy invasion was a trick and that the "real" attack was coming later in the Pas de Calais.

If this plan worked, the German high command would keep hundreds of thousands of troops tied down miles away from the main battlefield. When they finally realized that they had been deceived, it would be too late.

The Allies used every trick in the book. For every bomb dropped in Normandy before D-Day, two bombs fell in the Pas de Calais. Why, the Germans thought, would the Allies waste bombs if they didn't intend to land there?

But Ike's men went even further. They set up a fake army in southeastern England, at Dover, across the Channel from Calais. This First United States Army

Group, or FUSAG, was very believable. Ike's head-quarters announced that FUSAG was commanded by Major General George S. Patton. The Germans already knew Patton from the battles in North Africa and Sicily. He was a bold leader, and they were not eager to fight him again.

Everything was done to strengthen Patton's "army." Dummy army camps were set up. To make them look real

An inflated rubber dummy tank next to the real thing.

from the air, fake barracks were built, cooking fires were kept burning, and wash was hung on clotheslines. Wooden antiaircraft guns surrounded the camps. Tank tracks crisscrossed nearby fields, as if the "soldiers" were training.

Old planes no longer fit for battle were parked along fake runways. In case German spies prowled the countryside at night, loudspeakers blared records of bomber squadrons warming their engines.

Patton's "army" became like a gigantic Thanksgiving Day parade as rubber dummies were inflated, like Snoopy, and left where Germans could see them. Rubber tanks stood in fields row by row, just like the real things. Rubber LCIs and LSTs bobbed in the waterways around Dover. A youngster with a BB gun could have wiped out Patton's "army." The Germans would see enough of Patton's *real* army, the United States Third Army, after D-Day. But then they'd be too busy running to look at it carefully.

3

Countdown

Early on D-Day morning, June 6, 1944, General Eisenhower visited some American troops. These men, Ike knew, were jittery. Most of them would be going into battle for the first time against a well-prepared enemy. He still couldn't tell them much about the OVERLORD plan. But one thing he could say to make them feel better: "You needn't worry about the air. If you see a fighting plane, it will be ours."

The Supreme Commander knew what he was talking about. The air preparations for OVERLORD had begun years before. Scores of airfields had sprung up in England, until it seemed that the country would be paved over with runways. Airmen joked that you could taxi a bomber the length and width of the island without scratching a wing.

There were plenty of wings to scratch in England in 1943–1944. The RAF and United States Army Air Force had gathered over fifteen thousand aircraft for the invasion, the largest air fleet ever seen on the face of the earth. In addition to fifty-eight hundred bombers and five thousand fighters, there were thousands of troop carriers, gliders, seaplanes, camera planes, and artillery spotters.

This air fleet had one main job to do before D-Day: keep as many German soldiers and weapons as possible out of Normandy. This was a hard assignment. The Luftwaffe was one of the best weapons Hitler had. No invasion force had a chance with its planes overhead. OVERLORD had to take care of the Luftwaffe before anything else.

But how? The Americans had tried to bomb enemy aircraft factories in 1943. Not even winged battleships like the B-17 Flying Fortress and B-24 Liberator had succeeded against Germany's air defenses. Terrible battles were fought in the skies five miles above Germany.

As the bombers plowed ahead, yellow and black Focke-Wulf FW-190 fighters rose to meet them like swarms of angry hornets. Machine guns blazed. The black puffs of exploding cannon shells rocked the planes from side to side.

Soon the air was filled with trails of greasy black smoke, showers of sparks from exploding planes, and parachutes. Fighters and antiaircraft guns took a heavy toll. As many of sixty bombers, 600 airmen, were lost on a mission.

Things began to improve at about the time Ike be-

came Supreme Commander. Early in 1944, new United States fighter planes arrived in England in large numbers. The best fighter was the P-51. Nicknamed the "Mustang," it was fast and powerful, like a wild horse of the sky. It bristled with fifty-caliber machine guns, which fired bullets so large that they could knock down anything with wings. The bomber crews welcomed their "little friends," the tiny "peashooters" that protected them so well.

German airplane factories were heavily bombed, but not heavily enough to cripple the Luftwaffe. Something had to be done, and done soon, otherwise OVERLORD would be unable to control the air over Normandy.

Then, in March, 1944, the United States Air Force chiefs made a bold decision. The old posters at fighter bases had reminded the pilots: "Stay between the bombers and the enemy. It is not how many Germans you destroy but how many bombers you bring back that counts!"

These posters were taken down and thrown away. The new posters said: "Go after the Hun and destroy him wherever you find him!" ("Hun" was a slang name for "German"; it comes from the name of a tribe of barbarians that invaded the ancient Roman Empire and were especially cruel and destructive.) The Nazi fighter planes themselves became targets. As one hotshot Mustang pilot said: "If they don't come up and fight, we'll go

General Eisenhower addresses the crew of the battleship U.S.S. *Texas*, June, 1944. The Supreme Commander made it a point to visit every major unit slated to take part in the invasion.

down and shoot 'em on the ground. And if they go under-ground, we'll land and throw rocks down their holes."

Luftwaffe losses skyrocketed. From March to May, 1944, two thousand four hundred forty-two fighters were destroyed in action and another fifteen hundred through accident and other causes. Worse, the Nazis were losing experienced pilots faster than new ones could be trained to take their place. No doubt about it: OVERLORD would "own the air" over Normandy when the big day came.

With the Luftwaffe under control, Allied air power turned to its main job of protecting the invasion. Even with good weather, OVERLORD's planners needed fif-teen weeks after D-Day to build up an army in France equal to the forces Hitler already had there and in nearby Belgium. German reinforcements had to be kept away from Normandy during these weeks when the Allies were strengthening their manpower.

Look at the map and you will see that Normandy forms a natural box separated from the rest of France by several wide rivers. The Germans were sure to rush troops and tanks across these rivers once the invasion began. Here was the catch, for if the bridges over these rivers were cut, it would be as though the Germans were stranded on the far shore of a wide ocean.

The Allies began an "air blockade" using fighter-bombers. A fighter-bomber is a regular fighter plane loaded with one thousand pounds of bombs or more. Hundreds of American P-47 Thunderbolts and RAF Spitfires streaked across the Channel each morning. Soon every road to Normandy ended at a riverbank, where a jumble of twisted steel lay instead of a bridge.

A taste of things to come: waves of United States
Air Force B-17 "Flying Fortresses" drop tons of bombs
on German installations in occupied France to prepare
the way for OVERLORD.

The Germans tried to repair the collapsed bridges, but it was no use. Each time they began work, camera planes would fly over to keep tabs on how things were going. When repairs were nearly finished, the fighter-bombers returned.

OVERLORD's planners also knew that Rundstedt's forces needed 100 trainloads of supplies a day from Germany. Everything that had to do with railroads was bombed: tunnels, repair shops, freight yards, cross-overs, signals. Locomotives were a favorite target. A locomotive is big and blows up like a fireworks show when air-to-ground rockets hit its boiler. By May, 1944, over 900 locomotives had been destroyed. There would be times when one thousand freight trains stood waiting for locomotives to pull them. If they waited long enough, a locomotive wouldn't have to come, because the fighter-bombers found the trains as well.

Yet these successes came at a high price. From January through May, 1944, the Allies dropped two hundred fifty thousand tons of bombs on Nazi targets. Delivering these bombs cost them over three thousand nine hundred bombers and fighters shot down. Nearly twenty-five thousand airmen were killed or captured, or one man for each ten tons of bombs dropped. But without their sacrifice OVERLORD couldn't have gotten started.

The people of France aided the Allies in everything that had to do with OVERLORD. They were encouraged by a tall, thin, stubborn man who had escaped to England when the enemy took over. This man was a general, and he spoke over the radio, telling his countrymen not to give up hope. They must join together to resist the invader. They must prepare for the day of liberation. Posters with the general's words were secretly printed and appeared on walls in every city in the country. "France has lost a battle!" they said. "But France has not lost the war!" The general's name was Charles André Joseph Marie de Gaulle.

A secret army called the Resistance, or the Underground, formed. Men and women, even teenagers, worked for the Resistance. Each person did what they knew best. Some fought back in peaceful ways. They spread little jokes about "the Masters" to make the Germans look silly. They called the Germans "the Boche," meaning "the blockheads," because of their short haircuts. They chalked nasty slogans about them on the sidewalks. They tapped *dot-dot-dot-dash* as the Germans walked by; . . . — is Morse Code for the letter "V." And V is for Victory.

Some Resistance people spied on the enemy. Whenever they had information, they sent it to London by radio, carrier pigeons, or messengers who traveled back and forth across the channel along secret routes. Spying was dangerous work, and thousands of people were caught by the Gestapo, or Nazi secret police. The Gestapo starved and tortured prisoners for information, then shot them.

There were also thousands of armed Resistance fighters. The Allies sent many weapons into occupied France. BBC (British Broadcasting Corporation) broadcasts often ended with strange announcements. An announcement might say that "the orange trees will bloom tonight" or "Uncle Jean has found his goat." These were code messages telling Resistance groups when and where to wait for supplies.

Special squadrons of bombers painted black took off from secret airfields in England. The planes flew through the night until compasses told them they were near the right place. Looking down, the crew saw blinking flashlights from the ground. Out went the heavy boxes attached to parachutes. Rifles, pistols, machine guns, ammunition, grenades, radios, and medical supplies drifted quietly to earth. By May, 1944, over one hundred forty thousand French men and women were armed and ready to fight.

These Resistance fighters often used their weapons as D-Day drew near. German patrols were ambushed. Bombs made to look like lumps of coal exploded in the boilers of German troop trains. Telephone lines were cut.

The Nazis called the Resistance fighters "terrorists." French people called them "heroes" and "patriots." They did OVERLORD'S work and did it well.

By the spring of 1944, the OVERLORD clock was ticking faster and faster. Ike had set D-Day for dawn on the

General Charles de Gaulle ordered the French Resistance to be ready to cut communications and otherwise harass the enemy when the signal was broadcast from London. French fighters operating behind the lines tied up thousands of German troops, preventing them from joining the main battle in Normandy.

morning of June 5. Everybody and everything was ready. Nothing had been forgotten, from the largest battleship to a group of Sioux Indians from South Dakota. The Sioux would land in Normandy and radio important messages in their native language. Chances were that no German would be able to make sense out of their "code."

As the day drew near, the final countdown started. Excitement began to build. A strange nervousness filled the air. Common soldiers, even civilians who had never heard the word OVERLORD, felt it. Something was about to happen, and it would happen soon.

The normal secrecy of wartime England was doubled and redoubled. Ambassadors from foreign countries were not allowed to leave or enter Britain. Even their mail was opened and read by British intelligence agents. Anything that might refer to OVERLORD was cut out with a razor blade. The ambassadors didn't like this, but OVERLORD was more important than their letters home.

English people, too, began to feel like prisoners in their homeland. Ike had asked their government to close long stretches of the coast. He wasn't taking any chances. The armies were gathering along the coast for the trip to "the far shore" — Normandy. He didn't want people living in the area to leave, and maybe talk about what they had seen. Nor did he want strangers to see things they shouldn't.

Closing the coastal areas meant hardship for some people. Brides in some towns had to be satisfied with small wedding parties, for when guests from outside drove up to the roadblocks, they were met by mean-looking military policemen with submachine-guns and told to go home.

The soldiers began to move out of their base camps during the last week in May. The move came suddenly and without warning. One day a place was crowded with British and American troops. Next morning all was empty and quiet. It was like a dream. Only the tents remained. The men left so quickly that there wasn't even time to say goodbye to their families or friends. All they could do was write short messages on the tents' canvas walls. *"Sorry Jean. Had to go. Johnny,"* said one message. Did Jean and Johnny ever meet again? We hope so.

Day and night, columns of vehicles, some of them 100 miles long, rumbled toward the seaports along England's south coast. Quiet streets echoed with the grinding of heavy truck motors. The *clackety-clack* of tank tracks made it hard to sleep.

Lines of marching troops snaked along the highways. It was a beautiful month, that May of 1944. The air was heavy with the sweet perfume of wild flowers. Men stuck flowers into the netting of their helmets for good luck.

The sun beat down as the soldiers marched, sweating under their heavy packs. English people turned out to cheer them on. They didn't know where they were going, but they knew it was someplace important. They lined the roads, clapping and waving, weeping and wishing them Godspeed. Children gave the American OK sign, thumb and forefinger in a circle. "God be with you, young man. I remember the first war," an oldtimer kept saying. You could tell that his heart was breaking, for he wanted to be marching with them.

The troops who passed through Dorchester would always keep the memory of the priest who stood on a street corner. All day long he made the sign of the cross as each group marched by, and they bowed their heads.

Whenever the troops stopped to rest, housewives came out with jugs of tea and slabs of buttered bread. Food was scarce in wartime England, but people eagerly shared what little they had with the soldiers.

And so it went until the troops reached their new camps along the coast. The gates of the camps clanged shut behind them and were locked. Double coils of barbed wire surrounded the fences. Armed guards patrolled outside. Posters asked passersby "Please do not talk to the troops." Over two thousand Counter Intelligence Corps agents poked into everybody's business. There were even spies to spy on the spies.

Once inside these camps, no one could leave. A farmer discovered that the only veterinarian in the neighborhood was in a camp. He drove his sick cow up to the gate and asked the guard to allow it to be treated by the vet. The cow could be treated, the guard said, but wouldn't be let out. Some civilians asked what was going on inside another camp. They were invited to see for themselves; then the gate slammed shut. They were guests of OVERLORD until "later," whenever that was.

Things had to be done this way, for these camps

Getting ready to push off. Canadian troops go aboard their shark-mouthed LCIL (Landing Craft, Infantry, Light) before joining the main assault convoy.

were the soldiers' last stop on English soil. There they heard the word OVERLORD for the first time and learned of their part in it.

At last things began to make sense. OVERLORD was like a huge jigsaw puzzle, each piece of which joins many others. Now the men saw that their training ex-

Under the protective guns of the warship in the background, Allied LCTs (Landing Craft, Tanks) muster for the voyage to "the far shore"—Normandy.

ercises weren't games, but serious business upon which lives depended.

Soldiers saw that the town they had "captured" so often was an exact model of the French town pictured on the screen in their briefing hut. A group of tankmen saw why they had had to land on a certain English beach and no other; it was like a French beach called Utah on the maps.

British glider pilots learned their mission in a special way. A model of the area they would have to fly over had been built by the RAF. It was accurate even to the

height of the trees and the size of the houses. The RAF then made a film of the model and showed it to the pilots. Every landmark came into view as it would during the actual mission. After they had seen the film so many times that they knew it by heart, it was shown again, only this time through a blue filter. These pilots would have to fly into Normandy at night and had to spot landmarks by moonlight.

When the briefings ended, the men of OVERLORD knew that they wouldn't just be dumped on a beach and left on their own. They were part of a careful plan. Knowing this gave them confidence.

"The mighty host was tense as a coiled spring," Ike later wrote. By the morning of Saturday, June 3, the one hundred seventy thousand assault troops were aboard their ships, waiting. The last shell was loaded on the warships and they rode at anchor, waiting. Bombers stood on their runways like patient elephants, waiting.

Waiting. Waiting.

Waiting for the Supreme Commander to give the final order that would begin OVERLORD on the morning of Monday, June 5.

Men and machines waited for the order, but Mother Nature had other plans. She sent a storm that would have scared Noah.

OVERLORD'S commanders usually met twice a day to go over plans and talk about new problems. Soldiers keep late hours in wartime, and these meetings were held about four o'clock in the morning and nine o'clock at night. During the Saturday evening meeting, the weathermen gave Ike bad news. The beautiful weather was on the way out. On D-Day there would be thick clouds, high winds, and buckets of rain. Ike was shocked and wanted to wait a little longer before deciding what to do.

At 4:15 the next morning, Sunday, June 4, Ike met his commanders again. He had no choice now. The weather was getting worse by the minute and he called off the invasion for the next day.

Signals flashed to all forces in England: Freeze everything for twenty-four hours! Some convoys had already sailed when Ike made his decision. Since strict radio silence was in effect, fast destroyers sped after them with the news. By nightfall all the convoys except one had gotten the message and were heading back to port to ride out the storm. This missing convoy was sailing faster than the others and hadn't received the turn-back order. If it stayed on course, the Germans would see it and put two and two together. Anxious hours passed until a British seaplane found the convoy sailing at top speed straight for France and signaled it to go back.

Ike was worried. His broad smile was gone. His jaw was set and the muscles worked in his cheeks. The strain was terrific. He could put off the invasion for a day, maybe two days. But if the weather didn't improve, he'd have to wait two weeks for another try. Only then would the tides at Normandy be right again for a landing.

But waiting was dangerous. Many soldiers had been cooped up on transports for three days and were seasick. Allowing them back into England meant that news of OVERLORD might leak out. So many men couldn't be kept quiet forever.

A gloomy group of commanders met on Sunday

night to hear the latest weather report. The chief weatherman couldn't promise a miracle, but he could promise something. The weather would improve starting Monday afternoon, June 5, and last until Tuesday evening.

Silence. Nobody spoke after the weatherman finished his report. The *tick-tock, tick-tock* of the clock on the wall was the only sound in the room.

Ike broke the silence, asking his commanders what *they* would do. Montgomery spoke: "I would say — go." All agreed, but decided to wait a few hours longer before making a final decision.

The last meeting took place seven hours later, at 4:15 in the morning on Monday, June 5. Each officer said what was on his mind. They would be taking a big gamble, but going ahead with the invasion seemed safer than waiting another two weeks.

Ike looked at his commanders. They had never seen him so serious. Then he said, almost whispering, "Okay, let 'er rip."

Those in the room hurried out to give the starting orders. As they left, Ike called out "Good luck."

D-Day for OVERLORD would be the morning of Tuesday, June 6, 1944. Nothing in the world could stop the clock now.

A United States Coast Guard cutter pulls away from a jeep-carrying vessel after settling some last-minute business.

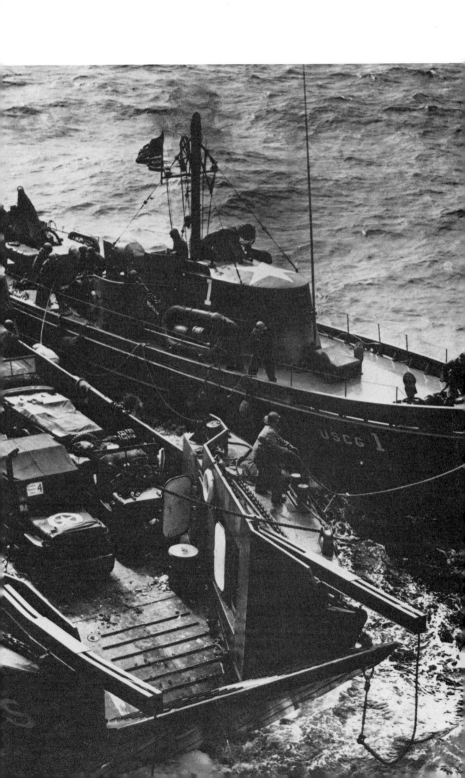

4

Assault from the Sky

The C-47 transports — some eleven hundred of them — were lined up on runways all over England. They stood in the twilight, waiting for the take-off signal from the control towers. Like every OVERLORD plane, they had black and white "invasion stripes" painted on wings and fuselage. These stripes were visible from the ground for easy identification, for no one wanted Allied planes shot down by their own trigger-happy ground troops.

It was the same aboard each plane. The men sat cramped together on hard, narrow benches on either side of the aircraft. Some laughed nervously. Others whispered. But most sat quietly, wrapped in their private thoughts.

The engines coughed, giving off puffs of smoke as

each plane lumbered up to the starting line. The pilot gunned the engines and the plane shot forward. Faster and faster it went, until with a soft *whoosh* it left the ground. Circling to gain speed, the plane climbed to altitude, where it joined others to form a V.

The Vs filled the sky, their red and green navigation lights twinkling like fireflies. For hours they streamed overhead. The pounding of their engines shook windowpanes in the darkened villages below. Each V, like a spearpoint, then headed south toward France and the coming battle.

The planes were soon swallowed by the night. A soft rain beat against the windows, while inside a pale orange bulb gave the only light. How strange it made the men look; how strange and *frightening.*

Their mothers would have had trouble recognizing them. Their faces were smeared with brown, black, and green paint. Some had their heads shaved, leaving only a tuft of hair down the middle, like an Iroquois brave's. This was no costume party, and everything had a good reason behind it. They darkened their faces to prevent their skin from reflecting the moonlight and giving away their position to the enemy. They made themselves look like savages to scare the enemy, hoping to make him lower his guard for a split second. In their kill-or-be-killed world, that split second could mean living or dying.

Each man wore a baggy camouflage suit with yellow, green, and brown spots, as on a forest floor. Pockets and pouches bulged with rifle and submachine-gun bullets; clips of cartridges were stuck into the linings of their steel helmets. Grenades dangled from their belts. Long fighting knives were strapped to their ankles. Coils of rope, spades,

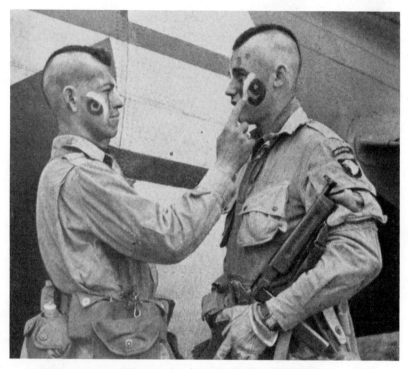

Two members of the 101st Airborne Division have shaved their heads like Iroquois braves and are putting on war paint. Unlike Iroquois, though, they carry Tommy-guns.

and pick handles stuck out of their packs or were wrapped around their waists. Each man carried at least eighty-five pounds of equipment.

These were proud men. They believed they were the best in their armies. And they were the best because they jumped. They were paratroopers.

OVERLORD called for parts of three United States and British divisions, about eighteen thousand men, to parachute into Normandy a few minutes after midnight on June 6. They were supposed to arrive in three waves. The first wave would be made up of a few dozen pathfinders. In addition to his regular equipment, each of these volunteers carried a sixty-pound bag with powerful lights and radar beacons. The pathfinders had to move fast once they landed. They had to find their way in the dark to places outlined on their maps and set up their lights and beacons to guide the main force. If the pathfinders failed, OVERLORD failed — it was that simple.

About half an hour later, the main force would begin to arrive. The beacons below would be the signal for thousands of paratroopers to "hit the silk." Their job was to dig in and clear a landing zone for the gliders, due to arrive in two or three hours.

Military gliders are giant motorless aircraft made of wood and canvas; these were larger than a C-47 transport. Because they have no engines, they must be towed at the end of a 900-foot nylon rope. Gliders can land in tight places, bringing equipment that cannot be dropped by parachute: jeeps, light tanks, antitank guns. The antitank guns would be worth their weight in gold on D-Day; for without them, the paratroopers wouldn't have a chance when the enemy brought up his heavy armor at daybreak.

The paratroopers' mission was to land at either end of Normandy. The United States Eighty-second Airborne ("All American") and 101st Airborne ("Screaming Eagles") divisions would land at the base of the Conten-

tin Peninsula, the "thumb," near Utah Beach. The British Sixth Airborne would land near Caen, a few miles inland from Sword Beach. The paratroopers would capture some key points, destroying others to keep enemy reinforcements away from the beaches when the seaborne invasion began.

The plan was risky. Nothing like it had ever been tried before. An airborne attack in broad daylight is always dangerous, because so many things can go wrong. A night drop, even with a full moon, is asking for trouble. Air Marshal Leigh-Mallory thought at least half the paratroopers would be killed on D-Day.

Ike still thought he had to take the chance and order the air drop. Yet he was worried: what if Leigh-Mallory was right?

One of the hardest things Ike ever had to do was watch some of the 101st take off. As his car rolled up, its four-star general's flag fluttering, the men were already boarding the planes. He went from group to group, stepping over baggage and wisecracking with the troops.

"Are you a good shot?" he asked one teenager. "Yes, sir," was the answer. "That's the stuff," said the supreme commander. "That's what will win for you tonight."

"Who is the toughest man in the outfit?" Ike asked someone else. A sergeant called out that they'd let him know after they'd been in Normandy for a few hours.

Ike says goodbye to some of the Screaming Eagles of the 101st Airborne Division. Notice the men's blackened faces.

"Good," he chuckled. "Send him back to me and I'll have something for him."

Ike stood watching the planes taxi to their starting lines. What was he thinking of just then? We'll never know. But far away, at the United States Military Academy at West Point, his only child, John, was due to graduate in a few hours. Maybe Ike was thinking about him. For as the planes soared into the darkness, tears filled his eyes. Generals cry too.

The first Allied troops to land in Normandy were sixty pathfinders of the British Sixth Airborne Division. As their transports neared the drop point northeast of Caen, German antiaircraft guns opened fire. Cannon shells exploded like strings of firecrackers. *PAM . . . PAM . . . PAM . . . PAM.* Steel splinters, shrapnel, beat against the planes' metal bodies like hail on a tin roof. Each splinter could rip through a person like a buzz saw.

The pilots began "jinking," weaving to dodge shells. That was a mistake, because some pathfinders had to jump out over the wrong places. It was exactly 12:18 A.M.

Hurry! Hurry! Hurry! No time to waste. The pathfinders rushed about in the darkness until they found one another and were able to place the signals.

Yet some never made it. Two men came down on the lawn of a beautiful old mansion. Too bad it was the headquarters of a German army division. Nazi officers who had been playing cards dashed out when they heard the planes pass overhead. "Where have you come from?" one shouted, pointing his pistol at the pathfinders. "Awful sorry, old man, but we simply landed here by accident" was the reply. Then they were marched off to spend the rest of the war in a prison camp.

But the Germans had already suffered their first D-Day defeat. As their antiaircraft guns were banging away at the British pathfinders' planes, three gliders pulled by three bombers slipped over the coastline unnoticed. Cutting their towropes, they swooped down quietly, like huge bats, toward two bridges a few miles away.

These bridges crossed the Orne River and a nearby canal north of Caen. Capturing these bridges would keep open the way from Sword Beach to Caen, which Montgomery wanted to take by D-Day evening.

The first glider touched down at ninety miles an hour, knocked over a cow, and skidded to a stop in front of the German guard posts. Moments later the other two gliders landed. Shouts filled the air. The password "Able-Able" was answered by "Baker-Baker" and "Charlie-Charlie."

The bridge guards didn't know what was happening. British troops leaped from the gliders. Some raced for the German positions, shooting and throwing grenades as they went. Others ran across the bridges to disconnect the dynamite charges which had been placed to prevent such a thing from happening. One group set up landing lights in the places indicated on their maps. It was so easy. In a few minutes the Allies had liberated their first corner of France.

At 12:50 A.M. the transports bringing the second wave, two thousand British paratroopers, thundered overhead like a runaway express train.

"Stand up and hook up," the jumpmaster of each plane shouted over the engines' noise. Every man sprang to his feet and hooked his static line to a bar that ran along the side of the plane to the door. That static line was his lifeline. For when he dived from the plane, it would jerk his parachute from its pack. If it didn't jerk it out completely or fast enough, it wouldn't open. Then he'd be the first person to reach the ground.

The planes headed for the lights outlining the drop zones. The British pilots had their hands full as the German gunners sent up curtains of antiaircraft shells. The unarmed planes couldn't protect themselves. All they could do was dash across the sky, between and through the deadly puffs of smoke that opened around them. "Jerry," their nickname for the Germans, was busy to-night.

A small red light gleamed next to each plane's open door. Two minutes to go. One minute. Thirty seconds. The wind whistled through the aircraft, but the men were too busy to think about the cold.

Then the light turned green. Go. "Out, out, out," shouted the jumpmaster. And out they went, head first. Anyone who froze at the last moment was "helped" out by a kick in the seat of the pants.

Hearts pounding, they fell through the velvety black-ness. A snap, and the parachute opened. A jerk, and the canopy caught the air, breaking the soldier's fall. Sud-denly blossoming white parachutes filled the sky.

The British paratroopers' battlefield began in the sky above Normandy. They were helpless as they drifted earthward, dangling in their harness. German flares arched upward to meet them, bathing them in a pale green light. Instantly tracer bullets cut flaming paths through the night.

It was beautiful, like having a bird's-eye view of a fireworks show. Yellow, green, blue, white, and red tracer bullets crisscrossed. Every fifth machine gun bullet is a tracer, filled with a chemical that burns in the air. The Germans used tracers to help each gun crew tell how it was shooting.

These beautiful colors killed men. Riddled bodies drifted gently downward. Planes were hit and exploded with a loud *whoof,* showering the paratroopers with flaming metal. Men hurtled by, their parachutes collapsed and burning.

"A miss is as good as a mile," they say. Some paratroopers had very near misses indeed. One man found four tracer holes through one pants leg, two through the other. A bullet had ripped off both of his breast pockets. There were holes in his backpack, and his parachute looked like a Swiss cheese. Yet he didn't have a scratch on him.

The paratroopers' drop zones were east of the Orne River. But the wind was strong, and pilots mistook the Dives River farther east for the Orne.

Rommel had flooded the flatlands around the Dives. Deep ditches filled with muddy water and stinking slime zigzagged through the area. Most of those who landed there were drowned when dragged under by their heavy packs and wet parachutes. Others landed in strange places, like the man who crashed through the top of a greenhouse, scattering glass all over the place and waking up the neighbors. One man made a pinpoint landing — right down a well.

Across the fields rolled the notes of hunting horns. There is nothing in the world that sounds like an English hunting horn at one o'clock in the morning. The horns blared, calling the men of the Sixth Airborne together. By twos and threes, by fives and tens, they slogged across the moonlit fields toward the horns.

Part of the force moved eastward, heading for the Dives. Five bridges crossed this little river, and they were blown up to keep German tanks from crossing. Meanwhile, other troops were clearing a landing zone for the gliders, due to arrive at 3:30 A.M.

A group of paratroopers led by twenty-nine-year-old Lieutenant Colonel Terence Otway had a special assignment. It was one of the most dangerous jobs given to any soldiers during World War II.

The village of Merville lies on high ground near the mouth of the Orne River. The Germans had placed a battery of four heavy coastal defense guns at Merville. The guns were aimed in such a way that they could fire down Sword Beach. This meant that the landing troops would be knocked over like bowling pins as soon as they left their boats.

The Germans had done everything possible to defend the Merville Battery. The guns were cased in steel and concrete. They were guarded by 200 soldiers in machine-gun nests and rifle pits. A minefield, two belts of barbed wire, and an electrified fence lay in front of the defenders' positions.

Otway had to destroy the Merville Battery. He

wasn't taking any chances. He planned to have heavy bombers soften up the target before leading his 750 men to the attack. But he was also working against time. For if the Royal Navy didn't receive a message that the guns were destroyed by 5:30 A.M., warships lying offshore would open fire. Anyone in the area, including Otway and his men, would be killed.

Otway's plan went wrong from the beginning. Of his 750 paratroopers, only 150 were able to make their way to the meeting point. The bombers missed their target and the gliders with his special equipment never arrived.

What a mess! Otway's men would have to attack heavily armed enemies across a minefield without mine-detectors, mortars, flamethrowers, and lightweight ladders. And they would be outnumbered.

Otway's force was in position by 4:30 A.M. It was quiet, so quiet that you could hear your wristwatch ticking. Someone with insulated gloves and wire cutters snapped the circuit of the electrified fence. So far, so good.

Just then a herd of dairy cows became frightened and stampeded, mooing loudly. The Germans opened fire and the British charged.

There was not time to cut the barbed wire. Otway's men blew pathways through the wire with explosives and dashed across the minefield. "Everybody in! We're going to take this bloody battery!" someone shouted.

Men stepped on mines and were blown to bits. The survivors kept running straight at the chattering machine guns. They fell, dead or wounded, and others took their place.

The Germans battled like the professional soldiers they were. But they were no match for the Tommies — British GIs — who came on without counting their losses. By 4:45 A.M. it was all over at Merville Battery. Otway had lost over half of his men; of the 200 Germans, 178 lay dead or dying.

With only minutes to spare, the Tommies blew up the guns by putting grenades into a pile of the Germans' own cannon shells. Then they ran for their lives in case their message failed to get through to the warships offshore. The whole attack had taken fifteen minutes.

Otway's gliders never arrived, but the Sixth Airborne's main glider train came in as planned. At 3:32 A.M., sixty-nine gliders dropped their towlines and dove steeply near the village of Ranville.

The men waiting below held their breath. If the gliders landed safely, the dangerous time would be over. They'd be able to hold off the Germans with the heavy equipment the gliders brought.

One glider, hit by antiaircraft shells, fell in a ball of flame. But the others came on, silently, except for the wind whistling over their wooden bodies.

The pilots steadied their gliders, pulling out of the dive. The stomachs of the men inside sank, their ears popped as in a high-speed elevator. "Hold tight!" a ser-

A field somewhere in Normandy. American C-47 transports have just released the towropes of gliders, some of which are circling, while others have already landed.

geant said. The men linked arms, took a deep breath, and lifted their feet off the floor. The ground came rushing up at them.

The gliders bounced and skidded as they touched down. The "Rommel's asparagus," which had been overlooked in the darkness, were knocked down. One after another, the gliders' wings sliced through the buried posts like matchsticks; luckily the enemy hadn't had time to mine them.

The sound of splitting wood and tearing canvas filled the air. Gliders bounced, bumped, and screeched to a stop. Some spun around wildly as a wheel collapsed, tipping them over onto a wing. Others flipped over onto their backs.

Shouting, cheering Tommies tumbled out of the gliders. "This is it, chum," one cried. "I told yer we wouldn't 'av ter swim."

The landing zone looked like a glider graveyard in the moonlight. It was spooky. Gliders lay with their noses buried in the ground. Broken wings and tails covered the fields. Yet things were better than they looked. Casualties were light, and forty-nine of the sixty-nine gliders were in good condition. Better still, their cargo was safe.

If a glider's door was jammed, the Tommies cut away the wooden fuselage with axes. In a few minutes shiny new jeeps, trailers, and antitank guns were ready for action.

The glider train also brought Major General Richard Gale, the Sixth Airborne's commander. Tall, red-faced, with a thick moustache and bushy eyebrows, Gale was a tough veteran of many battles.

Gale set out with his men toward Ranville. German soldiers were firing with their *Schmeissers* — submachine guns — forcing some paratroopers to dive into a roadside ditch. The general ordered them to get back on the road and move ahead. When they complained of the danger, a voice boomed over the noise of the battle: "Don't you dare argue with me — Richard Gale. Get on, I say, get on."

They did "get on." They captured Ranville. They carved out trenches with dynamite and their antitank guns were in place when the sky began to grow light in the east.

Daybreak was near, and so was the enemy. It had been a long night for the Sixth Airborne, but the day would be even longer.

The Americans were also busy early that morning. As the British pathfinders landed, pathfinders of the Eighty-second and 101st Airborne Divisions were leaping from their planes over the Contentin Peninsula fifty miles to the west. They were the first of over thirteen thousand Americans who would drop into Normandy during the next few hours. It would take 822 transport planes to ferry them across the English Channel.

The American paratroopers had several missions. The "Screaming Eagles" of the 101st, under Major General Maxwell D. Taylor, were to cut the main road from Carentan in the south, where the enemy had many troops and tanks. But their main task had to do with Utah Beach. Rommel had flooded the area behind the beach. The only way to move inland from the beach was over narrow pathways that led through the flooded area. These pathways had to be in American hands by the time the main force arrived offshore in the morning. If the 101st didn't capture them, the troops might be trapped on the beaches and wiped out by the German artillery.

The "All Americans" of the Eighty-second, under Major General Matthew B. Ridgeway, were to come down further inland. They also had two assignments. The first was to capture bridges over the Merderet and Douve Rivers, blocking enemy reinforcements from Cherbourg to the north. The second was to capture the town of Sainte-Mère-Eglise on the main road from Cherbourg to Carentan.

The Americans ran into more trouble than the British. Thick clouds covered the Contentin Peninsula, making it hard to locate the drop zones marked by the pathfinders. German antiaircraft gunners blasted away at the transports with everything they had. Many pilots were "green," this being their first time in battle. They were so scared that they only wanted to unload the paratroopers and get away.

The transports neared the drop zones and the paratroopers prepared to jump. A jumpmaster standing by an open door shouted: "Is everybody happy?"

"Hell yes!" came the reply.

One man murmured a prayer as he stood up: "Dear God, bless the men of this Division and let them land safely."

The paratroopers shouted "Geronimo" as they jumped. Then, like snowflakes blown by the wind, they scattered over a fifty-square-mile area.

Imagine what it must have been like to float down through streams of tracer bullets. Frightened men landed alone in the dark in strange places. They were lost. The roads and buildings they saw were nothing like the ones they had studied on maps and pictures.

Strange shapes loomed up at them out of the darkness. A paratrooper lay in a cornfield as a giant shadow moved toward him. Closer and closer it came, growing with each step. His hands shook and his teeth chattered, he was so scared. Just as he was about to open fire, the thing identified itself with a low moo.

Men assembled, aided by a one-cent snapper that made a sound like a cricket. Its *"click-clack"* was answered by *"click-clack, click-clack."* If it wasn't, a grenade or a burst of machine-gun fire followed.

One group had an experience they'd talk about for the rest of their lives. They had found one another in the darkness and were walking down a dirt road when they saw another group coming toward them. Someone snapped his cricket and thought he heard an answer. But as they came closer, they saw the shape of the other group's helmets. Germans!

The Germans must have made the same mistake, for the enemies recognized each other when only a few feet away. To open fire at such close range would have wiped out both groups. So they walked past each other, looking straight ahead, as if the others weren't there at all. They just kept walking until the darkness swallowed them up again.

The Eighty-second had more than its share of trouble. Many paratroopers landed in the swamps along the

Merderet and Douve; Rommel had flooded large areas around these rivers also. No one will ever know how many drowned, but all who were there told how, again and again, they saw their buddies disappear under the muck.

The lucky ones were able to get to their ankle-knives in time. Cutting off their parachutes and equipment, they struggled to reach solid ground. They were tired and in no shape to battle Germans.

German bullets zinged overhead. A man lay on his back trying to catch his breath and saw tracers flying two inches above his nose.

There was no time to wipe their feet and change their socks. They grabbed whatever guns they could find and joined the battle. Their feet squished in their wet boots. Nobody had a chance to change socks for three days. And they slept feet-to-head in their two-man fox-holes. It was not a pleasant smell, but a lot better than being with someone who fell into piles of cow manure, as some men did.

The wind blew twenty members of the Eighty-second away from their drop zone and set them down in the town square of Sainte-Mère-Eglise. They never had a chance. A building on the square had caught fire and the Germans ran to the spot just as the paratroopers landed.

It was like landing in a bonfire. Two men fell into the burning building and exploded as the flames set off the mortar shells they carried. The parachutes of others' caught in tree branches. The men hung there, helpless, as the Germans emptied their *Schmeissers* into them.

Private John Steele saw it all. His parachute had gotten caught on the church steeple and he dangled over

After the battle. An American paratrooper talks with French women after the liberation of St. Mère Eglise.

the street for three hours. He swung back and forth, playing dead, until the Germans cut him down and took him prisoner.

General Ridgeway and his assistant commander, Brigadier General James "Jumpin' Jim" Gavin, rounded up a few hundred men and headed for the Merderet and Douve River bridges. German tanks, though, had already beaten them there, and all the Americans could do was dig in to prevent them from crossing.

Sainte-Mère-Eglise fell at 4:30 A.M., becoming the first French town to be freed by the Americans. When the paratroopers reached the town square, they stopped in their tracks. They saw the bodies of their friends hanging from the trees by their parachute lines. "Oh, my God," said a colonel. Then he took out a battle-torn flag and ran Old Glory up the flagpole. Mission accomplished.

The 101st had an easier time than the Eighty-second, but not much easier. Its planes overshot their drop zones, sending some paratroopers drifting out over the English Channel, where they drowned. But most of the Screaming Eagles landed safely, although widely separated.

Men fought by themselves or in small groups. It was a bushwackers' battle, the kind of fight the frontier scouts in the old West had known. GIs and Germans hunted each other, Indian-style. They hid; they killed; they ran; and they hid again.

Sergeant Harrison Summers and Private John Camin became a two-man army. Armed with a submachine-gun and a rifle, they attacked a German camp behind Utah Beach.

They took turns. Summers charged into a house, cutting down four Germans with his submachine-gun. Then Camin broke into another house, doing the same with his rifle. After doing this a few times, they came to the last house in the row. Summers kicked in the door and found fifteen Germans eating breakfast; they hadn't heard the shooting in the other houses. They never finished their meal, for Summers shot them as they stood up. Summers and Camin had killed fifty enemy soldiers in less than a half hour.

By the time they finished, the Eighty-second's and 101st's gliders were arriving. Few of the big aircraft landed in one piece. Gliders plowed into trees, splashed down into rivers, and tore up planted fields. One bounced off the chimney of a house, dropped into the yard, flipped over and slammed into a stone wall, killing everyone aboard.

But most landed without loss of life. Paratroopers swarmed over the wrecks, saving whatever equipment they could find. Then they, like the men of the Sixth Airborne, dug in and waited.

The assault from the sky had taken the enemy by surprise. Everything seemed to be working in OVERLORD's favor and against the Germans.

The bad weather that had worried Ike so much made the Germans careless. The German soldiers in Normandy were tired. They had stood guard duty for many hours in May, when the weather was perfect for an invasion. The Allies had kept them awake for many more hours with a bagful of tricks. For example, boats with loudspeakers came near the shore at different places and blared recordings of ships' engines.

The German generals were happy about the bad weather. No one in his right mind, they thought, would risk an invasion at such a time.

They relaxed. Boat patrols were called in and the crews given some much-needed shore leave. Generals left the coast to attend meetings inland. Field Marshal Rommel went home to Germany for a few days; June 6 was

his wife's birthday and he wanted to be with her and their son at this joyful time.

The Germans didn't know what to think once the paratroopers began to land. Again an accident helped OVERLORD. The wind scattering the paratroopers over

This American glider was smashed to pieces when it landed, killing several airborne troops.

a wide area made it seem that many more men had been dropped and that they were everywhere at once. The Allies also dropped hundreds of dummies in uniforms. When the dummies landed, strings of firecrackers were set off to imitate gunfire.

The Germans were fooled into believing that the airborne invasion was a trick to draw them away from the real invasion area: the Pas de Calais. They wasted valuable time trying to decide what was happening. There was still no sign of ships off the coast. Yet excited cries of *"Fallshirmjaeger! Fallshirmjaeger!"* — "paratroopers! paratroopers!" — kept pouring into headquarters from every corner. Were these paratroopers part of a real invasion, or what? No one knew.

Von Rundstedt decided he had to do something. Whatever these paratroopers were doing in Normandy, they had no business being there. At 4:30 A.M. he ordered the Twelfth SS Panzer and *Panzer Lehr* divisions to attack at sunrise. The Allies would have a hard time defeating these soldiers. For the SS were not ordinary German army men, they were Nazis of the worst kind. Cruel in battle, they also ran Hitler's concentration camps, where millions of innocent people were murdered. The *Panzer Lehr* was also special. *"Lehr"* comes from the German word for "teacher"; this division's main job was to train others in methods of tank fighting. Both divisions had masses of heavy Tiger and Panther tanks.

There was only one problem with Rundstedt's order: he had no right to give it. He was commander-in-chief in the west, but he didn't control all the troops in the west. These two tank divisions belonged to a reserve force that only Hitler himself could order into battle.

But Hitler couldn't order anything that morning. He had taken a strong drug to make him sleep, and no one at headquarters was brave enough to wake him up. They were afraid that if they did, he would begin to yell and curse and beat the furniture with his fists.

Der Fuehrer slept his drugged sleep. Von Rundstedt's face turned bright red; he was so angry that he couldn't speak. His officers in Normandy ran around, not knowing what was happening.

And the paratroopers waited behind their antitank guns. They were in good shape after all. The Americans held the exits from Utah Beach and the town of Sainte-Mère-Eglise. The British held the Orne River bridges and Ranville.

The paratroopers waited and watched the eastern sky grow lighter. Then, about 5:30 A.M. the ground began to shake with explosions of bombs and shells. But they weren't from German planes and guns. "What next?" shouted a Tommy. "They're firing jeeps!" That is, the Allies were firing shells that were so large that they sounded like jeeps being hurled across the sky.

The main invasion had begun from offshore.

5

Neptune

Ike's order to "let 'er rip" had been like turning on the switch of a giant motor. Wheels began to turn, spinning faster and faster until it raced ahead at full power.

By 6:00 A.M. on June 5, the invasion fleet had raised anchor and was streaming out of its ports into the English Channel. Ships came from every harbor along the 250-mile coast from Plymouth to Land's End. The United States Twenty-ninth Division sailed from Plymouth. Those who knew their history remembered the Pilgrims, who had left from the same place 300 years earlier.

Never had there been such a fleet. It was made up of over five thousand ships of all kinds. There were coal-burning tugs and merchant vessels, ocean liners and hospital ships. The whole alphabet of special landing craft was there: LSTs, LCIs, LCAs. There were even a few wooden sailboats.

Warships — over 700 of them — stood guard. Fast PT boats darted about like water beetles. ("PT" is U.S. Navy shorthand for Patrol Torpedo boat.) Packs of sleek destroyers sliced through the water with their sharp-pointed bows.

Heavy cruisers plowed ahead, unhurried, as if on parade. They bristled with guns and had names like H.M.S. *Black Prince, Ajax,* and *Scylla.* The U.S. Navy was represented by the U.S.S. *Augusta, Tuscaloosa,* and *Quincy.*

The battleships moved even more slowly. They were the fleet's heavyweights and could afford to take their time. They towered above the water like floating castles, making the destroyers that surrounded them look like toys.

H.M.S. *Nelson, Ramilles,* and *Warspite* steamed ahead, their battleflags snapping in the breeze. U.S.S. *Texas, Arkansas,* and *Nevada* were old ships but proud, like sea queens. *Nevada* had been run aground in flames at Pearl Harbor, but she was on duty again today. All battleships had big guns, but some had super-big guns that could throw a two thousand-pound shell twenty miles.

All day and all night of June 5, the ships steamed along the English coast. As they passed, people watched them from the cliffs. Some knelt in prayer; others stood quietly. Ike was not the only person with tears in his eyes that day.

Yet the Germans saw nothing. Special OVERLORD ships jammed their radar early-warning system. Hundreds of Spitfires and Mustangs flew over the fleet and ahead of it. Their guns were "hot," and no enemy plane could fly near the fleet, let alone stay in the air long enough to radio a message.

The ships arrived at the assembly area south of the Isle of Wight near Southampton. This area was a ten-mile circle in the Channel that had been cleared of German floating mines by Allied mine sweepers. Each minesweeper had long saw-like wires, which it lowered into the water. When a wire touched the anchor rope of a mine, it cut it. The mine was then destroyed with gunfire.

The assembly area was nicknamed "Piccadilly Circus" after a famous traffic circle in downtown London. There each vessel took its place in one of the fifty-nine convoys bound for "the far shore."

The convoys sailed in five long columns. They resembled the spread fingers of a hand, one column for each of the beaches: Utah, Omaha, Gold, Juno, Sword. As the columns neared Normandy, the minesweepers cleared five more lanes. The extra lanes allowed the fast attack convoys to speed ahead of the slower support vessels, which wouldn't be needed until later in the battle.

The tiny minesweepers led the way. Behind them sailed the big warships and the floating command posts. These were five transports, one for each invasion beach, covered with forests of radar antennas and radio masts. Finally, there were the transports carrying the troops and their supplies.

Barrage balloons hover over a convoy carrying troops across the English Channel. These helium-filled balloons prevented enemy fighters coming too close to the fleet.

These transports stretched in an unbroken line from midchannel back to England. As the lead ships moved forward, others were leaving their docks to fill in the space. An antiaircraft barrage balloon attached to a steel wire bobbed over each ship. Low-flying enemy planes would either crash into the balloon or have their wings sliced off by the wires.

The trip across the Channel was no joyride. The storm had passed, but the wind still came in gusts, whipping up five-foot-high waves. Low clouds moved quickly across the dull gray sky.

The troops passed the time as warriors have always done before battle.

They played cards and read pamphlets about France and its people.

They sat with their backs to the wind, trying to write a last letter home while resting the paper on a helmet.

They slipped a picture of the wife and kids into a waterproof envelope for safekeeping.

They checked their weapons as though their lives depended on them. They did. The well-oiled sound of a sliding rifle bolt was like music; it meant the weapon wouldn't jam. Knife edges gleamed clean and sharp as they came off the whetstone for the last time.

The ships rose and fell, rose and fell, in the choppy waters. They seemed able to move in all directions at once. Nearly everyone except the sailors (and some of them, too) became seasick. Antiseasickness pills had been given out, but they made the cure feel worse than the illness. The pills had a chemical in them that caused the throat to tighten and made the mouth cottony dry. The best place for these pills was overboard, and that's where most of them were tossed.

Many a soldier missed his best army meal because of seasickness. OVERLORD's planners had made sure to stock up on special foods for the assault troops. Steak with eggs, chicken à la king, pork chops, ice cream and loganberries: a soldier could eat whatever he wanted and as much as he wanted.

Most men were too seasick even to look at food. Those who could eat, couldn't keep their food down. Men stood in line behind the ships' railings, waiting their turn to vomit over the side. Wars are not pretty for those who have to fight them.

Toward midnight on June 5, the fleet dropped anchor twelve miles off the Normandy coast. Everyone was tired, but no one slept. Who *could* sleep at such a time?

All was a blaze of light belowdecks, but pitch dark above. German soldiers stood in their watchtowers ashore, searching the darkness with powerful field glasses.

The hustle and bustle of last-minute preparations rang through the ships. Men shouted. Metal clanged. Wind whistled. Ships rocked back and forth.

At three o'clock in the morning of June 6, the first waves of assault troops took their places on the transports' decks. "This is it," they whispered among themselves.

They seemed more like packhorses than fighting men. Each soldier weighed nearly 300 pounds as he waddled across the deck; not even the paratroopers were so weighed down. The infantryman's combat boots alone weighed several pounds. Combat boots are not like hiking boots. The bottom is lined with a steel plate to protect the soldier's feet in case he steps on sharp booby traps planted in the ground. The boots' toes are also lined with steel, for kicking.

The steel helmet added more weight, as did the web belts hooked around the soldier's waist. These held pouches with as many as 250 rounds of ammunition, two water canteens, a first aid kit, a knife, a bayonet, and sometimes a pistol. Dangling from the suspenders that helped support the web belts were as many as ten explosive or smoke grenades.

A gas mask was kept in a sack at the soldier's side. The Germans hadn't used poison gas in battle so far, but there was no telling what a crazy man like Hitler might do if he felt cornered. A bulging knapsack held everything from a mess kit to dry socks and underwear.

Every man carried a gun. If he was lucky, he carried only a semiautomatic rifle like the American M-1. A "semiautomatic" is any gun that fires each time the trigger is pulled; a fully automatic weapon, like a submachinegun, fires as long as the trigger is held down and there is ammunition. The M-1 fired an eight-shot clip.

If he was unlucky, the soldier carried an extra weapon or part of a weapon. An infantryman might be one of a two-man BAR team. The letters stand for Browning Automatic Rifle, a machine gun that fires 500 shots a minute. One man aims the BAR and fires, while the other guides the belt that holds the bullets.

The infantryman might also be part of a flame-thrower team, a bazooka team, or a mortar team. The last two weapons gave the foot soldier the firepower of a small cannon. A bazooka fires a rocket from a barrel that looks like a piece of stovepipe. The rocket can't travel very far, but it can hit like a ton of bricks. It can burn its way through a tank's armor plate, exploding inside. A mortar is a tube that fires a shell at a steep angle, allowing it to reach over buildings, walls, and hills. A mortar shell explodes into hundreds of sharp splinters that travel through the air with the force of bullets. One mortar crewman carries the tube, the other the shells in sacks worn around the neck like a horse-collar.

Any of these packhorse-soldiers who fell into the sea would sink like a brick.

They had a long way to fall, for the deck of a troop transport rose twenty-five feet above the water. Acres of rope netting called "scramble nets" were draped over the ships' sides. The soldiers had to climb over the ships' railings and down to the waiting LCA assault boats. This was no time to be scared of heights.

Thousands of seasick, overloaded men swarmed down the scramble nets in the darkness. Below them the tiny assault boats bobbed in the swells like corks.

They were deadly "corks." A soldier had to time himself just right. If he let go of the net too soon or too late, he would fall into the water. Some men did fall, leaving behind only a few bubbles. Others had their legs crushed between the side of the transport and the assault boat. Or they cracked their skulls when they tumbled head first into the small boats below.

Canadians crowd into an LCI prior to setting out for Juno Beach.

Meanwhile, the ships' loudspeakers blared last-minute messages and battle cries.

"Get in there, Fourth Division, and give 'em hell!"

"Don't forget, the Big Red One [United States First Infantry Division] is leading the way!"

"United States Rangers, man your stations!"

As they were filled, the assault boats cast off and began circling the mother ships. The circles grew wider and wider as more and more boats joined the procession.

They were still circling when a strange sound began to come from the north, from the direction of England. The sound grew from a loud growl into a deafening roar. Wave after wave of RAF heavy bombers — eleven hundred thirty-six of them — swept through the darkness. The doors in their bellies slid open and six thousand tons of bombs rained down on the German shore defenses.

At 4:30 A.M. the American boats stopped circling. They formed into rows, their motors racing and belching puffs of white smoke. Then the signal came and they sped forward. The ten-mile dash to the beaches had begun. H-Hour (the moment they would reach shore) for the Americans would be 6:30 A.M.

Now began a living nightmare. The light assault boats pitched and tossed, bucked and rolled, in the rough sea. Waves broke over the boats' low sides, threatening to swamp them.

The boats' pumps couldn't work fast enough. Water poured in faster than it could be pumped out. The soldiers, already soaked with the cold salt water, had to bail with their helmets. Those who could, worked furiously. But many were too seasick to do anything. They just sat with their helmets between their knees, vomiting into them. Many lay on the floor, holding their bellies and moaning. It was awful.

The German beach defenders still suspected nothing. True, Allied bombers had been busy, and paratroopers were reported near Caen and Sainte-Mère-Eglise. But all was quiet on the beaches, except for the pounding of the waves.

The German troops changed their minds at 5:30 A.M., as the first rays of daylight began to outline the tall shapes in the distance.

Minutes passed. Lookouts gazed seaward, their eyes glued to field glasses.

Then they shouted to their comrades. The horizon began to fill, to come alive with ships.

Ships. Ships. Ships. There were more ships out there than they thought could ever be brought together in a single place. The sea seemed too small to hold them all.

"Here they are, the invasion fleet!" a German sergeant cried.

"But that is not possible," replied the lieutenant beside him. "That is *not* possible!"

It was not only possible, it was happening. At 5:35 A.M. German artillery at Utah Beach fired D-Day's opening shots out to sea. The gunners were shocked at the answer they received.

As the assault boats sped past the darkened battlewagons, hundreds of volcanoes seemed to explode at once from their sides. The naval bombardment had begun.

Battleship *Nevada*'s big guns open fire on Utah Beach.

The great ships had "buttoned up" for battle hours before. Hatches were locked and deck ventilators sealed to prevent any fires from reaching belowdecks. Everything that could fall or break loose was fastened or tied down. Wooden cabin doors were removed, for the blast that rushed through a battlewagon when her guns went off would splinter them. Everyone plugged his ears with cotton, for the rushing air could break his eardrums.

Ships' sides flared yellow and orange as their guns fired. *PAH-BOOM . . . PAH-BOOM . . . PAH-BOOM . . .* was all anyone on board could hear.

The ships seemed to lean back in the water each time they fired a salvo at the shore. The tornado of steel swept overhead at a rate of 200 tons of high explosive shells a minute.

The assault boats raced ahead under this protective canopy. The vibrations of the big guns punched the soldiers in the ears like a hard fist. Clouds of burned gunpowder drifted across the water. It made the men's eyes run and stung their nostrils.

But no one seemed to mind. Frightened, seasick assault troops stood in their boats and cheered. For what they smelled and saw seemed to them like victory.

The naval bombardment brought misery to the defenders of the Atlantic Wall. Fountains of earth leaped dozens of feet into the air whenever a shell landed, and they were landing often. Clouds of cement dust choked the German soldiers; beach sand crunched between their teeth.

They lay in their trenches with hands clasped over their ears. One German officer learned about the invasion when some large-caliber shells blew him out of his bed.

The assault boats kept coming, closer and closer, toward the beaches. Suddenly at 6:00 A.M., another sound was heard. It grew louder, drowning out even the rolling thunder of the ships' guns.

The sky filled with thousands of United States Army Air Force planes. Flying in closely packed formations, they zoomed over the fleet. Ignoring the shells from the fleet, fighters attacked anything German they could locate.

High above the fighters, the four-engined bombers —thirteen hundred sixty-five Flying Fortresses and Liberators — prepared to "drench" the beach defenses with high explosives. Their 500-pound bombs fell in long "sticks," making a shrill whistling sound. A newsman named Robin Duff watched the bombs hit from an assault boat. "The beaches shook and seemed to rise into the air, and ships well out to sea quivered with the shock."

The assault troops laughed, and cheered, and cried. A veteran of the fighting in the Pacific said: "By the time they had finished not even a rabbit could have been alive on those beaches."

He was wrong. The Germans were not rabbits, but tough soldiers who knew their business. Plenty of them survived the shelling and bombing. And they fought back.

The first Americans came ashore at Utah Beach. Among the assault troops of the first wave was Brigadier General Theodore Roosevelt, Jr., assistant commander of the Fourth Division.

It was strange to see General Roosevelt there that morning, armed only with a walking stick and a pistol. In olden times generals charged into battle with their troops. In modern times it is unusual for a general to lead an attack. Not that generals have become cowardly. Instead, it is that too much depends on a general nowadays; too many men look to him for orders for him to risk his life.

But Theodore Roosevelt, Jr., was no ordinary general. He came from a family of fighters and leaders. "Teddy" Roosevelt, his father, had led the Rough Riders in the Spanish-American War. "Teddy" later became our twenty-sixth President. The general's cousin was President Franklin D. Roosevelt.

At fifty-seven, General Roosevelt was "too old" to lead assault troops; he'd be the oldest man on the beaches. That's what his superiors said. Besides, he had a weak heart and arthritis in his shoulders. Pain shot through his body whenever he moved his arms.

General Roosevelt was not the sort of man to take "no" for an answer when he thought he was right. Those were "my boys" going into battle, and he wanted to be with them no matter what happened. He argued until General Bradley said he could go along. That was one of the smartest moves "Brad" made for D-Day.

The Utah Beach plan called for LCTs to launch thirty-four amphibious tanks. These would swim ashore in time to give covering fire to the assault troops.

But things went wrong, as they usually do in war. The inflatable "bloomers" that had to keep the tanks afloat collapsed in the rough sea. Many tanks went under, taking their crews with them. One LCT dropped its ramp onto an unswept mine. The explosion that followed tossed the lead tank a hundred feet into the air. Only twelve amphibious tanks reached the shore to cover General Roosevelt's infantrymen.

Losing most of the tanks was bad luck, but from then on the Americans' luck changed on Utah Beach. Drifting smoke from the naval bombardment hid the landmarks the assault boats were supposed to steer toward. A strong current also carried them a mile south of the planned landing place.

Both errors were the best things that could have

happened. The correct landing place was strongly defended. Had the troops tried to land there, they would have been cut to pieces. Instead, they landed at one of the weakest places in the Atlantic Wall.

Yet there were casualties. Boats sank and men drowned. Light enemy gunfire killed others. "I was just coming out of the water," one man remembers, "when this guy exploded right in front of me. There wasn't anything left of him."

A shell burst in the middle of a group, knocking down twelve men. Seconds later a lone nineteen-year-old stumbled through the smoke. His face was black and he walked like a zombie. General Roosevelt ran up to him and put an arm around his shoulders. "Son," he said gently, "I think we'll get you back on a boat."

The general soon realized that they had landed in the wrong place. He now had to make one of the most important decisions of D-Day. Another thirty thousand men and three thousand five hundred vehicles were due to come ashore in the next few hours. But where? Should he send them down the coast as planned, under the enemy guns? Or should he allow them to land fairly safely in the "wrong" place? Whatever he did was a gamble, for the troops would have to capture the exits off the beach. And they'd have to do it soon, otherwise men and equipment would pile up, making good targets for the German guns.

General Roosevelt decided to take his chances in the wrong place. "I'm going ahead with the troops," he told an aide. "We're going to start the war from here."

The Roosevelt luck held. As he led the troops forward to enlarge the beachhead, the second and third waves brought engineers and bulldozers. The engineers cleared channels through the underwater obstacles. The bulldozers carved pathways toward the exits that led across the flooded areas behind the beach.

The Americans flooded ashore with the rising tide. By afternoon a full division and its equipment — tanks, trucks, jeeps, field guns — was ashore on Utah Beach. General Roosevelt was everywhere, ordering them about at the top of his voice.

His infantry moved inland cautiously. Patrols inched their way toward roadblocks and machine gun nests. Then they broke into loud cheers and ran the rest of the way. The Fourth Infantry had joined hands with the Eighty-second and 101st Airborne.

By nightfall they had a beachhead five miles deep. This beachhead had cost the Fourth far less than anyone had expected: 197 dead and wounded. Another sixty men were missing and probably drowned.

Things didn't go that well at Omaha Beach twelve miles to the east. There the First and Twenty-ninth Divisions fought one of the fiercest battles in American history. By day's end "Bloody Omaha" had taken its place beside Gettysburg and Antietam.

The plan was for tank-supported troops to land on a steeply rising beach backed by high sand dunes. Behind the sand dunes were cliffs rising straight up from the beach. The highest cliffs — 170 feet — stood like towers on either end of the beach. Winding through the gaps in the cliffs were four steep, narrow paths leading inland. The Germans had turned this natural fortress into a death trap. It was one of the strongest places in the entire Atlantic Wall; for if they could keep the invaders off this beach, the Germans could slip between the Allied armies and cut them off. Soldiers call this a "flanking" movement.

Every inch of the offshore waters, the beach, and the beach exits was defended. Rommel really went all out at Omaha Beach. Minefields, barbed wire entanglements, dragon teeth, rocket launchers, cannon, machine guns: everything was ready to greet the "Amis," as they called the Americans.

And it would be a hot reception. These weapons were manned by some of Hitler's best soldiers. The 352nd Infantry Division had fought in Russia. Its officers and men thought the "soft" Americans would fall like wheat at the harvest. So let them come!

They came. And the Germans' boast almost came true — *almost*. Yet the Nazi "supermen" had forgotten one thing in their planning: the courage of the American fighting man.

The attack was to be led by sixty-four amphibious tanks, thirty-two tanks per division. As soon as the First Division's tanks left their LCTs, they were tossed about by the high seas. The pounding waves collapsed their "bloomers," sending twenty-nine to the bottom. The other three were saved only because the ramp of their LCT jammed and they couldn't be launched.

The Twenty-ninth Division's tanks all made it safely to shore. The navy men, seeing what had happened to the others, ran their vessels onto the beach rather than float the tanks in the killer surf.

But the damage had been done. Loss of the First

The cliffs of Omaha Beach loom in the distance as
American troops climb out of their assault boats and
begin to wade toward the shore under enemy fire.

Division's tanks cost hundreds of extra casualties along
its section of Omaha Beach.

Meanwhile, the assault boats rushed full speed ahead
toward the shore. The naval bombardment crashed overhead. Flat boats fired thousands of rockets from the steel
tubes that crowded their decks. The rockets shot forward,
pointing fiery fingers into the dawn sky. They sounded
like the cracking of giants' bullwhips.

The bombardment began to lift as the assault boats neared the shore. The navy men stopped firing, because they were afraid that some shells would land on the GIs. Such accidents had happened before and would happen again.

The assault boats sped on, coming closer, always closer, to the shore. The soldiers could see clouds of dust swirling on the beach ahead of them. They tensed, expecting the enemy's guns to begin firing at any moment.

Yet they were silent. Could they have *all* been destroyed? Maybe, the GIs thought. They prayed that the guns were destroyed.

Their prayers went unanswered. When the assault boats were about a thousand feet from the shore, the Germans opened fire with everything they had.

WHEEE-WOOMPF . . . WHEEE-WOOMPF. . . . WHEE-WOOMPF.

German artillery shells screamed overhead and exploded among the speeding boats. The first shells missed, throwing columns of water into the air.

But the enemy guns soon began to find their mark. Assault boats took direct hits and flew apart in a burst of flaming splinters. The force of the explosions blew men out of their laced combat boots.

Living and dead floated together in the water. Wounded men yelled to the passing boats for help. But they wouldn't stop — they *couldn't* stop.

Those beaches ahead were their only reason for being here. If they stopped to rescue a few men and failed to reach the shore, or to reach it on time, OVERLORD might fail. And so with tears running down their cheeks, the boatmen steered straight ahead.

As they came closer other sounds were heard. Machine gun bullets *PING . . . PING . . . PING*ed off the boats' metal sides. The *CLUNK* of mortar bombs filled the air.

The ramps of the assault boats flopped down 100 yards offshore. The boats couldn't go any closer because of sand bars. The troops had to walk the rest of the way in water up to their waists.

They stepped out of the assault boats into the cold sea. They were in the open, unable to defend themselves. Each man was weighed down by his pack and equipment.

He held his weapon over his head to keep it dry.

The machine gun bullets stitched the water all around them.

BRHHH . . . BRHHH . . . BRHHH . . . The sound of automatic rifle fire came from every direction.

Men fell forward one at a time or in groups of five or six. Soon the water around each man was colored by a spreading patch of red.

Exhausted men stumbled through the surf. They fell on the beach and lay there panting, like runners who have pushed themselves too hard.

All the while the Germans raked the shoreline and the beach with automatic weapons fire. Men lay in the open, hugging the ground as bullets whined inches above their heads. Others found shelter behind the dead. Still others gave up on the land altogether; they crawled back to the sea and hid behind the offshore obstacles. One man took cover behind a floating mine, which he held onto with all his strength.

Not only were the invaders' lives in danger, they were just plain uncomfortable. All D-Day uniforms had been treated with a chemical to protect the skin from poison gas. The chemical made the clothing stiff and itchy until it got wet; then it became soggy, and slimy, and smelled to high heaven.

The naval bombardment has lifted, but clouds of smoke and dust swirl around the cliffs behind Omaha Beach. The assault troops are perfect targets for the Germans hidden in their steel and concrete bunkers. *(next page)*

One group of GIs was having a harder time than even those on the beaches. OVERLORD agents had learned that the Germans had placed six huge cannnon on top of the cliff at Pointe du Hoe three miles west of Omaha Beach. These guns had to be knocked out on D-Day morning for the same reason the British Sixth Airborne had to destroy the Merville Battery.

General Bradley gave the job to the Second U.S. Army Ranger Battalion, commanded by Lieutenant Colonel James E. Rudder. He couldn't have given it to a finer group of men in any army. The Rangers are the American version of the British Commandos. All volunteers, they are specially trained in using explosives and in making surprise raids behind enemy lines.

To reach the Pointe du Hoe guns, Rudder's Rangers would have to climb a cliff as high — 117 feet — as a ten-story building and as steep. The Germans on top would do everything they could to stop them.

"It can't be done," one of General Bradley's officers said. "Three old women with brooms could keep the rangers from climbing the cliff."

Maybe so, but they'd have to give it a try. As two destroyers blasted away at the cliff's top, the rangers dashed ashore from their assault boats. Reaching the base of the cliff, they fired rockets carrying grapnels attached to rope ladders. Grapnels are small anchors with six hooks at the end for grabbing and holding.

The grapnels hooked into the top of the cliff and the Rangers began to climb. Now the real battle began. The Germans came out of hiding and rolled grenades down the cliff. They leaned over the edge, firing their

Schmeissers. They cut the ropes and kicked some of the grapnels loose.

Rangers fell, smashing themselves on the rocks below. But others rushed to take their places. In five minutes the first ranger bellied over the edge of the cliff. Others followed him, their rifles blazing. They rushed the "guns," then stopped in their tracks, not knowing what to think. For instead of huge cannon, they found six telephone poles pointing out to sea.

What had the Germans done with the real guns? Rudder sent a patrol to search the area and find out what had happened. The patrol found the guns hidden in a clump of trees and destroyed them.

Those guns had cost the Rangers a lot. Of the 225 men who came ashore, only ninety were left by nightfall. But they had saved hundreds of their buddies on Omaha Beach.

Down there everything was still a bloody confusion. The second, third, and fourth waves landed, only to stall at the water's edge. Dead, dying, and wounded Americans were everywhere. Bodies brought in by the tide joined the living along that terrible shoreline.

Saving lives became more important than fighting. Men in the water pushed the wounded ashore ahead of them. Those who had reached shore crawled back into the water to save others from drowning.

Many soldiers couldn't do anything. They were in shock, like someone who has been in a bad accident. Cold and dazed, they could hardly think or move. One youngster sat up at the water's edge while machine gun bullets

Aerial view of Omaha Beach showing assault boats stuck
on sand bars and men and equipment gathered on
the beach.

whipped up the sand around him. He just sat there, tossing
pebbles into the water and crying softly, like a hurt child.

"Medic!" "Medic!" The wounded called for help.

The Medical Corpsmen were the only ones who had to move around while the others took cover. The wounded were all over the beach, and they had to help them as best they could.

The Medical Corpsmen fought their war armed only with bottles of blood plasma, bandages, and injections of painkiller. They were as heroic as any paratrooper or Ranger. Nineteen-year-old Alfred Eigenberg found a soldier with a deep cut running from his knee to his hip. All he could do was give the wounded man some painkiller and close the wound with safety pins.

The combat engineers also had dangerous work: they had to clear the obstacles to allow ships with heavy equipment to unload near the shore.

The engineers were a favorite German target. The decks of their landing craft were piled high with boxes of explosives and coils of fuse. Enemy mortar rounds scored direct hits, killing everyone on some engineer boats.

Those engineers who made it ashore attached dynamite to the obstacles. Yet sometimes they couldn't blow them up, because men were still hiding behind them, too afraid to go to the beach.

German sharpshooters "helped" the engineers blow up the obstacles. They let them place their charges, then opened fire. A single rifle bullet could set off the explosives, killing a five-man engineer team.

The German commander at Omaha Beach thought he had won the battle. The Americans were finished, he thought. "The American invasion is stopped on the beaches," he radioed Rundstedt. "Heavy losses are being inflicted on the survivors. The beaches are littered with burning vehicles and dead and dying troops. Heil Hitler!"

The Nazi had spoken too soon. After hours of terror and shock, of bleeding and dying, a strange thing happened on Omaha Beach. Individual Americans decided they had had enough and took matters into their own hands. By word and example, they rallied small groups of fighters. Courage, like defeat, is contagious.

Colonel Charles D. Canham of the Twenty-Ninth Infantry stood up and began to move among the troops huddled on the ground. A bloody handkerchief was tied around his wounded wrist. "They're murdering us here!" he shouted over the noise of the gunfire. "Let's move inland and get murdered!"

Down the beach, Colonel George A. Taylor of the First Infantry had the same idea. "Two kinds of men are staying on this beach," he yelled, "the dead and those who are going to die. Now let's get the hell out of here."

An old top sergeant said it differently. "Get your ass up that hill!" he bellowed in his best parade-ground voice.

Soldiers stood up, moving forward and upward toward the enemy positions. Navy fire-control teams had come ashore by then with radios to direct ship-to-shore gunfire. Those big shells made all the difference to the battle-weary foot soldiers.

"Get on them, men! Get on them!" Rear Admiral C. F. Bryant called to his gun crews on the battleship *Texas*. "They're raising hell with the men on the beach, and we can't have any more of that! We must stop it!"

And stop it they did. Turning broadside to the shore, mighty *Texas* let go with everything she had. Destroyers whipped in so close to the shore that their keels scraped the sandy bottom. Their guns became so hot that sailors had to stand on top of the turrets with fire hoses to cool them down.

"Thank God for the navy!" came a message from the beach.

The troops climbed the narrow paths in the teeth of German machine guns. But mines were a more serious problem. The cliffsides were filled with them; and removing them was slow, dangerous work. A "point man" led the way on his hands and knees. With a bayonet he gently probed the ground ahead. When the point scraped against the metal side of a mine, he cleared the sand and carefully lifted the explosive, placing it to the side of the path. If there was no time for this, he simply marked the mine with a piece of colored paper.

Many mines could not be located. Men stepped on them and died. Yet some were lucky — *very* lucky. Everyone held his breath when a sergeant, running down a path, stepped on a mine that was lying uncovered in the open. "It didn't go off when I stepped on it going up, either," he explained. It was a dud.

By 1:30 P.M. the worst was over on Omaha Beach. General Bradley received a short message that told the whole story: "Troops formerly pinned down are now advancing up heights behind the beaches." By evening they held a beachhead six miles long and less than two miles deep. But they were ashore and dug in, ready for anything.

Omaha Beach cost the United States Army two thousand five hundred killed, missing, and wounded.

"Thank God for the Navy." Navy communications
teams like this made it possible for the battlewagons
offshore to lay down accurate barrages with their big
guns to clear a path for the infantry.

The British beaches ran for twenty miles from the village
of Port-en-Bessin in the west to the mouth of the Orne
River in the east. The British Fiftieth Infantry Division

The second wave comes ashore on Omaha Beach. A beachhead has been secured, making it possible for the LCIs (Landing Craft Infantry) to unload their hundreds of troops near the beach.

would land at Gold Beach, the Canadian Third at Juno Beach, and the British Third at Sword Beach. There were also groups of French, Norwegian, and Polish soldiers with the British forces. These had escaped when Hitler captured their countries at the beginning of the war.

H-Hour for the British was 7:30 A.M., an hour after the American landing. The delay was due to differences in the tides along the Normandy coast.

The later landing was a good thing, allowing the Royal Navy to bombard the beaches longer. The sailors needed the extra time to aim carefully, for the British beaches had no high sand dunes or cliffs behind them. They were wide and flat. French houses and small towns

Canadian infantrymen came ashore at Juno Beach with their bicycles; they expected to travel fast and far on D-Day.

were built just behind the high-tide line. The assault troops, some of them, would land in people's front yards.

The British troops could count on large numbers of tanks at the beginning of the battle. They needed these tanks more than the Americans. For besides the usual enemy weapons, they would be facing whole divisions of German tanks.

The area inland from the British beaches was flat and open: tank country. Field Marshal Montgomery expected the Germans to counterattack with masses of tanks once they got over their surprise at the invasion. The British had to be ready for them with tanks of their own.

"Monty" had his way. Amphibious tanks blazed the trail ashore on D-Day. Closely behind them came LCTs bringing regular tanks and "Funnies." Having lots of tanks right there on the beaches saved countless British lives.

The mood of the British infantry was also different than the Americans'. Many soldiers were seasick after the rough channel crossing. German mines blew up landing boats. German gunfire knocked men down like pins in a bowling alley. Yet the British were both grim and gay at the same time. They were grim, because they remembered. They remembered the bombing of London and a hundred defeats at German hands. Now they were going to "give it 'em back." Revenge, giving the enemy a taste of his own medicine, was what they were out for.

And that's what made them gay. The Americans went into battle silently with their jaws set. The British went in with music. Their ships blared recordings of

"Roll Out the Barrel," a popular drinking song, over their loudspeakers:

> *Roll out the barrel,*
> *We'll have a barrel of fun.*
> *Roll out the barrel,*
> *We'll have the blues on the run.*

Tommies stood up in their assault boats and sang old army songs as shells crashed around them.

They went into battle calmly and with a sense of humor. A captain of the Royal Marines, noticing the obstacles near his speeding boat, quietly told the skipper: "I say, old man, you really must get my chaps on shore; there's a good fellow." His "chaps" came ashore with their bicycles, for the Royal Marines meant to travel fast and far on D-Day.

A sergeant and his men were dumped into the surf off Gold Beach when their boat sank. They lost their equipment and had to swim ashore under heavy machine gun fire. "Perhaps we're intruding; this seems to be a private beach," said the sergeant.

One band of warriors had a special mission. They wore no steel helmets, because such things weren't "manly." Instead, each man wore a green beret tilted at a smart angle. These men belonged to the First Special Service Brigade — British Commandos.

Lord Simon Lovat, their leader, was in a hurry. "Shimy" Lovat had promised his friend "Dickie" Gale to reinforce his paratroopers at the Orne River bridges by noon on D-Day. Lovat was a Scotsman, and Scotsmen like to be prompt.

The Scots also like the high-pitched wail of bagpipes even in battle. It "settles the nerves," they say. And among the first commandos to leave his assault boat was William Millin, Lovat's bagpiper. "Give us 'Highland Laddie,' man!" Lovat shouted as Millin stood in water up to his armpits.

Millin slogged ahead, bagpipes screeching and bullets zinging. He stopped at the water's edge, piping the commandos ashore. As they rushed by, one turned and said, "That's the stuff, Jock." ("Jock" is Scots slang for a country boy.)

At about 1:00 P.M. the men of the Sixth Airborne thought they heard bagpipes. Bagpipes! "No, couldn't be," they thought. They had been fighting for more than twelve hours. They were so tired that they *should* have been hearing strange things and seeing them too.

Yet the sound continued. It grew louder and louder, until everyone recognized bagpipes screeching "Blue Bonnets over the Border," an old Highland war tune. And up the road came Bill Millin at the head of a column of commandos.

The Germans were amazed. *"Verrückt! Verrückt!"* — "crazy, crazy" — they mumbled, shaking their heads. But they stopped shooting long enough to allow the paratroopers to greet the commandos. There was much handshaking and backslapping. Lord Lovat only looked at his watch and apologized for being "a couple of minutes late."

The people of Normandy greeted the invaders with open arms. Such happiness, such good feelings, hadn't been seen in these parts for four years.

"*Vive les Anglais,*" "Long live the English," they shouted as the Tommies went by. Ignoring snipers, they ran out to hug and kiss the soldiers. They offered them wedges of creamy, mellow Camembert cheese and jugs of Calvados, the fiery apple brandy of Normandy.

Some French people couldn't wait for the soldiers to reach them. They rushed down to the beaches to greet them as they poured out of the assault boats. The mayor of the little town of Colleville-sur-Orne put on his official uniform and welcomed the British on Sword Beach.

It was the same wherever the Americans went, too. Apple brandy, bread, butter, cheese: the French had hidden them from the enemy, and now they begged their liberators to eat.

The GIs knew they were welcome by the way the French treated their dead. An American had been shot along the road near a house. The farm couple came out, and while the wife watched, her husband covered the body with flowers and knelt in prayer.

A dead paratrooper lay on a bed in the best bedroom of a farmhouse covered from head to foot with the sweet wild flowers of Normandy.

The German dead were left where they fell. They didn't belong to France.

"*Vive l'Amérique!*" "*Vive la France!*" "Long live America!" "Long live France!" They cheered and cried, raising their fingers in the "V" salute. And they tapped . . . — again and again. V-for-Victory.

And the Germans? Their leaders slept through the most important hours of D-Day.

A French farmer says a prayer over the flower-covered body of a GI who fell in the road near his house.

Rommel had been awakened at 6:30 A.M. to be told about the paratrooper landings. He hung up the telephone, saying they were not serious; the weather was too bad for an invasion.

He changed his mind when his headquarters called him again, at 10:15 A.M., to tell of the landings along the coast. "How stupid of me. How stupid of me," he said as he hung up. He ordered his car and began the long trip back to France.

Der Fuehrer also woke up at about 10:00 A.M. He sat in his pajamas listening to aides describe the invasion.

But he was in no hurry. First he bathed and ate breakfast. Then he went over the morning's regular business. He had a long, leisurely lunch. Finally, in the afternoon, he gave Rundstedt permission to use the Twelfth SS and *Panzer Lehr* divisions from the reserve. The divisions didn't receive their marching orders until 4:00 P.M., twelve hours after Rundstedt had alerted them for battle.

The only German tanks to counterattack on D-Day belonged to the Twenty-first Panzer Division stationed near Caen. Its tanks moved out in the afternoon toward a gap in the British line between Juno and Sword Beaches. If they broke through, they'd be able to roll along the water's edge and destroy the invaders from the rear.

But it was too late. The Twenty-first's tanks began to roll, their drivers and crews eager for battle. As they moved forward, they ran smack into the massed fire of British antitank guns.

The sun was setting when the panzer troops heard the drone of airplane motors. British gliders, hundreds of them, unhooked from their tows and came down in the fields between the Twenty-first Panzer and the sea. The tanks would never be able to break through now.

Late that night some German tankmen stumbled along a back road. They were drunk and singing at the top of their voices. An officer watched, but didn't try to stop them. He watched, shook his head, and said "The war is lost." He knew.

D-Day was over. It had been a surprise to everyone.

The Germans were surprised; they thought concrete forts and bad weather would keep them safe.

OVERLORD's planners were also surprised, but pleasantly. In a secret report they had said that at least ten thousand Allied soldiers would be killed on D-Day. No more than three thousand lost their lives. Total casualties — dead, wounded, prisoners — were less than twelve thousand. But nearly one hundred thousand others had made it ashore safely.

D-Day was over. The battle of the beaches had been won. The battle of France was about to begin.

6

Breakthrough

The world learned about the invasion in different ways. At exactly 9:32 A.M., June 6, radio programs in Britain were interrupted by a simple announcement: "D-Day has come."

The news spread like wildfire. Housewives opened their windows and shouted to people in the streets below. Church bells rang and complete strangers stopped to congratulate each other.

Americans received the news in the middle of the night. On the west coast they heard it at 12:33 A.M.; on the east coast at 3:30 A.M. People who were going to bed late, or who had to get up early for work, turned on their radios. Soon they were calling their friends. Across the nation telephones rang and light switches were flicked on.

New York taxi drivers pulled up to the curbs and gave the news to passersby.

The night shifts working in the great war plants heard the news over loudspeakers. Men and women put down their tools and knelt on the dirty floors to pray.

Later that morning we children in that part of New York City called the Bronx made bonfires in the street out of fruit boxes. We "roasted" Hitler, Rundstedt, Rommel, and the whole Nazi gang.

At 10:00 A.M. President Roosevelt broadcast a prayer from the White House. No one who heard him will ever forget what he said and how he said it. For he put into words what millions of people were feeling in their hearts:

Almighty God: Our sons, pride of our nation, this day have set upon a mighty endeavor, a struggle to preserve our republic, our religion and our civilization, and to set free a suffering humanity.
Lead them straight and true; give strength to their arms, stoutness to their hearts, steadfastness to their faith . . . .
Thy will be done, Almighty God, Amen.

By the morning after D-Day, the Normandy beaches had become the world's largest junkyard. The wreckage of battle was scattered everywhere. It was as though men and machines were tiny dolls shaken out of a giant toybox.

Broken tanks, burned-out trucks, and half-sunk boats littered the beach and the offshore waters.

Under new management. Although captured and out of commission, this German fort and its gun still look wicked.

Soldiers' packs and personal belongings were scattered for miles around. There were socks and Bibles, toothbrushes and razor blades, chocolate bars and packs of matches. Here and there a broken banjo or tennis racket lay in the sand.

The saddest things were the letters from home and snapshots of loved ones. "Dearest Johnny . . ." ". . .

love Judy." ". . . the kids miss you . . ." The papers blew along the beach like autumn leaves, only they were stained with salt water and blood.

The beaches had to be cleaned up — *fast!* The war couldn't wait. There was so much to do and so little time in which to do it.

While the armies battled inland, the men on the coast were fighting the battle of supply. The Allied buildup had to be faster than the enemy's, otherwise they might be thrown back into the sea.

The buildup began at sunup on June 7. There were many more ships to be seen than even the day before. The sea off Normandy crawled with ships. It seemed, said a Royal Marine, "as if all the ships in the world were concentrated there." And far out to sea the sky was black with the smoke of more ships creeping over the horizon.

The Mulberry artificial harbors were already being towed into place and sunk. But the buildup couldn't wait for them to be ready. Instead, landing boats were run right up onto the beach to unload.

Beachmasters, navy men trained to direct traffic, gave orders over loudspeakers. "Hello, LST 1789. Pull alongside LST 1918 and unload when you're ready."

Bow ramps dropped with a splash and tanks, jeeps, trucks, trailers, and guns poured out of the ship's belly.

The morning after. Barrage balloons cover the swarms of LSTs unloading their cargos at one of the American beaches on June 7. More ships extending as far as the eye can see, wait their turn to unload. (*next page*)

Within fifteen minutes they were lined up on the beach and ready for battle.

Time meant lives and it couldn't be wasted. If a truck stalled, a bulldozer, the kind that can push over a house, towed it out of the way in seconds.

The world's largest junk yard, the Normandy beaches the day after.

The traffic on the roads leading inland was like rush hour around a major factory city. On an ordinary day fifteen thousand vehicles passed a check-point; that is, one vehicle every five seconds.

If the roads were too narrow or curvy to handle the traffic, the bulldozers moved in. They would knock down walls and level gardens to widen a turn. Or they tore down houses and cut through apple orchards to break up traffic jams.

Men and supplies came into Normandy in a steady stream. The buildup was so large that not even Mother Nature could stop it. On June 19–20, the worst channel storm in fifty years wrecked the American MULBERRY. Yet in less than two weeks the Allies had landed about six hundred thousand men and one hundred thousand vehicles.

German reinforcements couldn't keep up with the OVER-LORD buildup: the French people and the Allies' air force saw to that.

Early on D-Day morning General de Gaulle broad-cast a call to arms. "The simple and sacred duty of [France's] sons . . . is to fight with everything they have. They must destroy the hated enemy, the dishonored enemy who has crushed and sullied our homeland."

De Gaulle's words were the signal for the Resistance to swing into action. Its freedom fighters blew up enemy supply dumps and cut communications. They dynamited bridges and blocked roads, forcing the Germans to make long detours. On D-Day alone they interrupted railroad service 950 times.

Some Germans, like the Second SS Panzer Division, behaved like criminals and cowards. Ordered to move to Normandy from southern France, the Second SS was slowed up by the Resistance. The soldiers became furious. But since they couldn't trap the Resistance, they decided to punish innocent people instead. One day SS troops sur-rounded the village of Oradour-sur-Glâne and killed every man, woman, and child they could find.

OVERLORD's air power crippled the German

counterattack. The Allies put up a fighter umbrella from the English coast to central France. The pilots joked that there were so many Allied aircraft in the air at the same time that "you almost had to put your hand out to signal a turn."

To save time and fuel, the Allies decided to move their fighters and fighter-bombers to Normandy as soon as possible. Air engineer units came ashore behind the assault troops. By D-Day evening they were building emergency landing fields.

The engineers worked day and night. If there was a shortcut, a faster way to get something done, they found it. Sometimes they turned a stretch of paved roadway into a fighter strip. But usually they had to clear a site with bulldozers. After leveling it, they put down long sections of steel matting that looked like a honeycomb, which they covered with earth and packed down with steam-rollers. By June 19, all American and British fighter-bombers were operating behind the front in Normandy. Until then, relays of planes from English bases patrolled the English Channel and the invasion area. They were greatly needed and much-appreciated by the Allied ground troops.

During the first few days after D-Day, the German panzer troops were glad to receive their marching orders. They were eager to get into the fight. In the good old days they had rolled over one country after another. Now the Allies would be a pushover, they thought. They'd show them how German "supermen" made war.

"Little fish!" said the commander of the Twelfth SS

Panzer Division. He was sure this troops would throw the Allies back into the sea the morning after they arrived in Normandy.

General Heinz Guderian, who had led the German tank forces in Russia, told the commander of the *Panzer Lehr,* "with this division alone you will throw the Anglo-Americans back into the sea."

At first the panzers traveled in broad daylight, without air cover. Tanks, self-propelled guns, gasoline trailers, and troop-carrying trucks stretched for miles along the French highways. All went well until the sound of racing airplane motors split the air.

The planes came screeching overhead at treetop level. Machine guns rattling, United States P-47 Thunderbolts plastered the columns with thousand-pound bombs. Or maybe it was a swarm of RAF Typhoons firing streams of armor-piercing rockets. The Typhoon was the best tank-killer of World War II. The airmen called it "the can opener."

The planes did their work and did it very well. The Twelfth SS Panzer Division lost half its armor in a day. The *Panzer Lehr* was shot to pieces in a few hours.

Best of all, the murdering Second SS Panzer Division was made to pay for Oradour. The Resistance radioed for RAF Spitfires and in a few days the Second SS had lost four thousand men. Its commander wrote in a secret report: "The Allies have total air supremacy. . . . Our territory is under constant observation. . . . The feeling of being powerless against the enemy's aircraft . . . has a paralyzing effect."

A cold fear came over the German soldiers. *"Jabos"*

British "Typhoon" fighters were known as "can openers," because they were so heavily armed with guns, bombs, and rockets that they could destroy an enemy tank as easily as opening a tin can.

— Allied fighter-bombers — became the most terrible word in their language. Driven off the roads by day, the German tankers hid in the forests. Traveling only after dark, they hoped the *Jabos* wouldn't come over and drop flares.

Their hopes were dashed. Broken guns and burnt-out tanks lined the roadsides wherever they went. Many crews simply walked away from their tanks when they ran out of fuel. A fifty-five-ton Tiger tank was a "gas guzzler," using as much as three gallons to go one mile.

Not even individual soldiers were safe. Men caught in the open were chased by eight-gunned Thunderbolts. Sometimes pilots came down "on the deck"; instead of shooting at a German, they tried to cut him down with a wingtip. Even if the soldier escaped, he would dream about his close shave for years to come.

German soldiers began to ask *"Wo ist die Luft-waffe?"* — "Where is the air force?" Hitler's once-mighty air weapon was too busy trying to save itself to help the infantry. The troops in Normandy had to do their best without air support.

On D-Day only two fighters rose to meet the invaders. Flying low over Sword Beach, they fired a couple of machine gun bursts and ran for safety. The Germans had neither the pilots nor the planes to match the Allies. Every day their air fields were strafed by squadrons of low-flying fighters. Ground crews hid the surviving planes in the woods, but the *Jabos* found them there too.

A captured German soldier explained that the army had a new system of aircraft identification. "If we see silver planes, they are American. If they are colored, they're British. If we can't see them at all, they're the *Luftwaffe*."

Yet the Allied armies could not advance at lightning speed. Hitler had ordered his soldiers to fight for every foot of ground, and they obeyed, even though the odds were against them.

On June 7, Montgomery's forces advanced from Gold Beach to capture Bayeux, their first important French town. But his main attack stalled in front of Caen, the key to eastern France. Between Caen and Paris lay only 120 miles of open country, perfect for tanks. The Germans knew Caen's importance and prepared for a long battle.

The Americans also had their problems. They were fighting in a part of Normandy called the *"bocage,"* or "hedgerow country." A hedgerow was an ancient earth wall about five feet high. Weeds, thorn bushes, and trees grew out of each wall as thickly as in a jungle. For hundreds of years the Norman farmers had used hedgerows to fence their cattle and protect their crops from sea winds.

Thousands of hedgerows surrounded thousands of fields. The Germans dug into the hedgerows, making themselves invisible in the brush. But they could see the Americans coming, and their machine guns were ready.

Capturing each hedgerow meant fighting a separate battle. Planes weren't much help, because they couldn't spot the enemy from the air. In the slugging match that followed, the GIs had to dig out the "Jerries" one at a time.

It was dirty, dangerous work. German snipers were everywhere, and they had nasty tricks. They hid in the hedgerows with a few days' supply of food, a high-powered rifle, and plenty of ammunition. As the GIs went by, they shot them in the back.

Snipers often fired wooden bullets. Using these didn't mean that Germany was running out of lead. Snipers used them when firing toward their own lines. Being wood, they carried only a short distance and couldn't harm their own troops if they missed a GI.

Snipers surrendered as soon as they ran out of food and ammunition. They came out with their hands up, calling *"Kamerad"* — "friend." The GIs hated them because they were sneaky. They soon learned how to find snipers *before* they thought of surrendering.

Booby traps were another enemy trick. The Germans booby-trapped anything an Allied soldier might touch. Wine bottles exploded in men's hands. Taking a juicy red apple from a tree set off strings of land mines. Some soldiers had the shock of their lives when they pulled the flush-chains of farmhouse toilets. The Germans even booby-trapped their own dead. They knew Allied troops would have to bury them to prevent disease and saw nothing wrong with killing an enemy at such a time.

A clever GI might make the fear of booby traps work for him. During one battle a soldier found a nest of twelve eggs. There was no time to take them, so he scribbled a note on a board and propped it against the nest. "Booby trap," the note said. After the battle he went back to the nest and had a fried-egg party all by himself.

ENGLAND

LONDON

Portsmouth   Dover

Plymouth

NETH.   GERMANY

BRUSSELS   Cologne

Lille   BELGIUM

INVADED
JUNE 6, 1944

Dieppe

Laon

FORTIFIED AREA

Rhine R.

Cherbourg

St-Lô   Caen
Mortain   Falaise
          Argentan   PARIS

Seine R.

Moselle R.

Nancy

Brest

Troyes

Belfort

Lorient
Quiberon
St. Nazaire   Nantes

Orleans

Tours

Loire R.

F R A N C E

SWITZ.

Bay
of
Biscay

La Rochelle

Limoges

Lyon

ITALY

Bordeaux

Garonne R.

Rhône R.

Toulouse

Nice

Bayonne

Marseille
Toulon

INVADED
AUGUST 15,
1944

THE BATTLE OF
FRANCE

Mediterranean Sea

SPAIN

Miles
0   50   100

0   Kms.   100

© 1962 A. Karl/J. Kemp

There was no glory in this kind of fighting. War, for the infantry, is only dangerous and uncomfortable.

Living conditions that no civilian in a civilized country would stand for were a normal part of the foot soldier's life. He didn't like these conditions, but there was nothing he could do about them.

Soldiers ate because they were hungry, not because they liked the food. Since it was difficult to bring hot meals to troops at the front, they had to live on cold "K" rations. "K" — for "combat" — rations came in three cardboard containers, one for each meal. Breakfast was meat and vegetable hash. For lunch the soldier ate meat and vegetable stew. Supper was dried pork sausage and vegetables. There was also a candy bar, dry crackers, powdered coffee, and chewing gum. That was it.

One never felt full after a "K"-ration meal. Soldier-food was dull and tasteless. "The only way to achieve variety," a lieutenant said, "was to eat the ["K" ration] box instead of the contents."

The soldiers fought under the blazing sun. Sweat ran down their faces, down their backs, down their underarms. There was no place or time to wash in combat. They stank like billy goats.

OVERLORD's planners had thought of everything except mosquito nets. After all, they were invading France, not some Pacific island. Yet the mosquitoes of Normandy were often worse than in the Pacific. At sunset the men saw columns of mosquitoes reaching 300 feet into the air above the treetops. These columns were everywhere, and each contained millions of insects. They were hungry and they ate — GIs. They drove the troops crazy with their never-ending buzzing and biting.

"Sack-time" — sleep — was more precious to the combat soldier than the best food or even a bath. War is a twenty-four-hour-a-day business, every day. There is no time out for rest at the end of a day's fighting. Men stayed awake, if they wanted to stay alive.

Soldiers slept when they could, where they could, usually in a different place each night. The lucky ones had a roof over their heads. They might bed down on the filthy floor of a barn or in a damp basement with mice running about. But at least they were indoors.

The unlucky ones slept outdoors in holes in the ground. If it rained, that was just too bad; there was no place else to go. The rain beat down, filling the holes with cold mud. Yet the men slept, because they were exhausted. One man made an excellent pillow out of soft "earth." He slept peacefully, like a baby, on that wonderful pillow. In the morning he noticed that the "pillow" was a pile of horse manure.

The unluckiest men of all couldn't even lie down to sleep. On long marches they dozed off as they walked. They slept with their eyes open, while their legs kept moving.

On June 12, the Americans took Carentan, which lay on the main road to Cherbourg. They advanced slowly, but they advanced; that's what counted.

The Germans fell back in good order, making them fight for every village and town along the way. After a while these places began to look alike to the GIs. Clouds of dust hung over them after the artillery bombardment. The streets were broken piles of smoking wreckage with shattered glass littering the pavements. Doors and shut-

Streetfighting. After a while, one wrecked French town looked like any other to the GIs.

ters banged noisily back and forth in the wind. Stray dogs whined as they ran around looking for their masters.

The Americans were fighting in the streets of Cherbourg by the end of June. It was a savage battle in which every street was a front line and every house a fortress. Finally, on June 27, the Germans surrendered.

The city lay in ruins. The docks and loading cranes along the waterfront were wrecked, the warehouses heaps of smoking rubble. But the Allies had their first major seaport and would have it in working order in a few weeks.

They also had batches of German prisoners. Most of these men had been drafted into their country's army and suffered through the war like any GI or Tommy. They fought well, but surrendered rather than fight to the death. One man said it all, in *three* languages: *"The guerre — nicht bon"* — "The war, it's no good."

You could tell the real Hitler followers by their attitude. They acted as if they were winning the war and not the other way around. A German officer was brought in for questioning and the first thing he demanded was his personal servant. When told that the man was dead, he became angry. "Who is going to dig my foxhole for me?" he shouted. The tired, mud-stained GIs just looked at each other and grinned from ear to ear.

General von Schlieben, commander of Cherbourg, was even angrier. He complained about the "uncivilized" way the Americans treated a person of his high rank. He was used to sleeping in comfortable beds and eating the best restaurant foods. Now the Americans were making him stay in a drafty farmhouse and eat "K" rations. And when his trunk from Cherbourg fell out of a truck and burst open, souvenir-hunting GIs stripped his uniforms of the gold braid and buttons. When General Bradley heard the German's story, he was not heartbroken.

The area behind the Allied lines, meanwhile, seemed ready to burst. The buildup continued as men and supplies arrived by the shipload. By July 1, a million men had landed, along with one hundred seventy-seven thousand vehicles and five hundred thousand tons of supplies. Ike's commanders were ready to break out of the beachhead and destroy the German armies.

Montgomery's forces finally took Caen on July 9.

Already the top German commanders knew the Allies couldn't be beaten anymore. During a telephone conversation with Hitler's headquarters, Rundstedt gave the

Light tanks and armored cars have just been unloaded at a prefabricated pier that has been towed across the Channel and set up at Normandy.

best advice he could. Germany was finished; "Make peace, you fools," he snapped. "What else can you do?" Hitler fired the old man and gave his job to Field Marshal Günther von Kluge.

It made no difference. Things now began to happen fast enough to make the Germans' heads spin. On July 18, the Americans captured Saint-Lô. At last they were out of the hedgerows and bound for open country.

Two days later, July 20, the war nearly ended in a couple of seconds. As Hitler sat down to a meeting at his headquarters, a bomb exploded under the table. It had been put there in a briefcase by army officers who wanted to kill *Der Fuehrer* and end the war before it was too late. Four men were killed, but Hitler escaped.

Hitler took his revenge upon the hundreds of German officers suspected of being in the plot. These men were tortured and executed. Although Rommel had been wounded and was unconscious in a hospital when the bomb exploded, Hitler suspected him as well. A few months later (October 14) he was told that if he committed suicide, his wife and son wouldn't be harmed. He took poison and was dead a few minutes later. That's how Hitler rewarded the services of his most famous commander.

On July 25, the big Allied push began near Saint-Lô. The ground shook for hours as thousands of warplanes unrolled "bomb carpets" on top of the enemy lines. High explosives rained down until the German positions seemed to rise in the air in clouds of dust.

When the bombing stopped, part of the United States First Army under General Joseph Collins burst through the opening they had made. Collins's nickname was "Lightning Joe," and he deserved it.

Collins moved fast and hit with everything. His artillery stood wheel to wheel, pouring a steady fire into the Germans. The commander of one all-black artillery battalion had a favorite war cry. After each salvo he shouted toward the Germans, "Hitler, count your men." There were fewer men to count each time those guns spoke.

Collins's tanks charged forward. The general's voice could be heard over the din of battle, crying "Get along, there, tanks, keep pushing."

Collins's attack was followed up on August 1 by General George S. Patton's U.S. Third Army. If Collins was "Lightning Joe," Patton was "Hell on Wheels." Of all the American and British generals, the Germans feared him the most. With his two pearl-handled pistols, he felt at home on the battlefield.

Patton's army burst out of Normandy like a bolt of lightning. His armored columns sliced south and east into open country, grinding up whole German divisions as they went. Each tank column had air controllers equipped with radios. Whenever the tanks ran into heavy resistance. they stopped while the controllers ordered an "air strike." A few minutes later they were racing on as before.

Patton was not interested in capturing territory. He wanted to move behind the enemy armies, trapping them and destroying them. Fast, faster, fastest: these were General Patton's watchwords.

The Third Army traveled about forty miles a day. It moved so swiftly that it outran its maps. To solve the map problem, mobile printing plants raced along with the army. Every few days they turned out thousands of new maps, in eight colors, to let Patton's commanders know where they were.

Hitler became the best general on the Allies' side. He wouldn't let his officers fight their battles as they thought best. He was a "military genius," he thought, and interfered with their plans. And he made a mess of things.

Hitler's worst mistake was to order an attack when he should have ordered a retreat. While his forces were busy attacking the Americans near the town of Mortain, Montgomery and Patton set a trap. The British and Canadians moved south from Caen toward Falaise. The Americans moved north from Argentan. Between them they caught the Germans in the "Falaise pocket."

As the pocket closed, the Germans tried to escape. From August 13–19, marching troops and their equipment jammed the narrow roads leading from the pocket. The columns moved at a snail's pace, sweating and cursing under the summer sun.

The Allied pilots showed them no mercy. They were angry, especially after learning that the Germans were using the Red Cross insignia on trucks carrying troops and weapons.

Two or three planes would seal off the front and rear of a column with bombs. Then the squadrons lined up, one after the other, and came screeching over the Germans ten feet off the ground. It was like shooting fish in a barrel. They couldn't miss, and the Germans had no place to hide. If a tank broke out of line and tried to escape across an open field, a Typhoon or Thunderbolt swooped down and finished it off.

Germans surrendered by the thousands. Yet many refused to give up, or let others leave the battle. The SS shot other Germans in the back as they ran toward the GIs with white flags and hands raised above their heads.

"Old Blood and Guts" was the nickname of General George S. Patton, Jr., whose Third Army led the American breakout from Normandy.

Falaise broke the back of the German armies in Normandy. In addition to ten thousand killed and fifty thousand captured, they lost over 500 tanks and countless trucks, field guns, and other supplies. Field Marshal von Kluge was so upset by the defeat that he took poison. In his suicide note he begged Hitler to end the war as soon as possible. "The German people have suffered so unspeakably that it is high time to put an end to this frightfulness!"

But Hitler wouldn't listen; the war continued, and so did the German defeats. On August 15, a few days before the Falaise pocket closed, there was another D-Day, this time in the south of France. Using North Africa as a base, the U.S. Seventh Army under Lieutenant General Alexander Patch and forces loyal to General de Gaulle crossed the Mediterranean Sea and landed near the great seaport of Toulon. These landings were nothing like Omaha Beach. There was no Rommel or Atlantic Wall along the Mediterranean. German resistance was light, and by nightfall the Allies had put ashore ninety-four thousand men and over eleven thousand vehicles at a cost of 183 men killed and wounded.

Battered by Patton in the north and by Patch in the south, the Germans began a general retreat. On August 25, American troops marched into the "City of Light," Paris. Next day Patton wrote to the Supreme Commander: "Dear Ike, today I spat in the Seine (River)." On September 11, one of Patton's armored columns linked up with Patch's army near Dijon, forming a single, unbroken Allied front.

The battle of France was ending; the battle of Ger-

Paris at last! French girls welcome the first American troops into Paris, August, 1944.

many was about to begin. It would be a hard-fought battle, but one whose outcome was certain.

On April 30, 1945, eight months later, Adolf Hitler sat in a secret room beneath his headquarters. Berlin, his capital, was burning from end to end. He put a pistol to his head and pulled the trigger. A week later, May 7, Germany surrendered unconditionally.

World War II in Europe was over. It ended exactly eleven months and one day after General Eisenhower gave the order to begin OVERLORD.

This peaceful scene is part of the invasion fleet off the coast of southern France a few hours after the initial landing.

The wind blows on the Normandy seashore. It whistles through the ruins of the Atlantic Wall that still overlook the beaches.

There is some rusted barbed wire here and there, and sometimes a child finds a broken rifle in the sand.

Above Omaha Beach there is an American ceme-

tery where many who fell on D-Day are buried. There are long rows of white grave markers and a beautiful chapel

Into the heart of Hitler's "Thousand-Year Reich." American armored columns cross a captured bridge over the Rhine River into Germany.

where visitors may sit quietly and think. There is a lot to think about.

But except for these relics and monuments, Normandy is as it has always been.

The cows crop the grass and give their delicious milk.

The orchards in late summer burn with the redness of apples.

People go about their business in peace.

Peace. Yes, that's what OVERLORD had been about from the beginning.

Some More Books

BELFIELD, E. M. G. AND ESSAME, HUBERT. *The Battle for Normandy.* Philadelphia: Dufour, 1965.

CARELL, PAUL. *Invasion — They're Coming! The German Account of the Allied Landings and the 80 Days' Battle for France.* New York: E.P. Dutton & Co., Inc., 1963.

EISENHOWER, DWIGHT D. *Crusade in Europe.* Garden City, New York: Doubleday & Co., Inc., 1948.

HARRISON, GORDON A. *Cross-Channel Attack.* Washington, D.C.: Office of the Chief of Military History, Department of the Army, 1951.

MARSHALL, S. L. A. *Night Drop: The American Airborne Invasion of Normandy.* Boston: Little, Brown & Co., 1962.

RYAN, CORNELIUS. *The Longest Day, June 6, 1944.* New York: Simon & Schuster: 1959.

STANFORD, ALFRED B. *Force Mulberry: The Planning and Installation of the Artificial Harbor off U.S. Normandy Beaches in World War II*. New York: William Morrow & Co., Inc., 1951.

WILMOT, CHESTER. *The Struggle for Europe*. New York: Harper & Brothers, 1952.

WRIGHT, GORDON. *The Ordeal of Total War, 1939–1945*. New York: Harper & Row, 1968.

Index

airborne divisions
  British: Sixth Airborne,
    75, 77–85, 91, 133
  United States: 82nd ("All
    American"), 73, 85–91,
    112; 101st ("Screaming
    Eagles"), 73, 85, 91, 112
Air Force, United States
    Army, 51, 53
Argentan, France, 162
"Ark," Armored Ramp
    Carrier, 42
army divisions:
  British, Third Infantry, 129
  Canadian, Third Infantry,
    129
  German, 352nd Infantry,
    113; see also *Panzer*
    (tank) divisions
  United States, First
    Infantry, 105, 112, 113,

125; Fourth Infantry,
    105, 109; 29th Infantry,
    97, 112, 113, 125
Atlantic Wall, 11–13, 18

BBC, British Broadcasting
    Corporation, 57
bazooka, 103
Berlin, Germany, 165
bocage, see hedgerow country
bombers, Allied, B-17 Flying
    Fortress, 51, 109; B-24
    Liberator, 54, 109
booby-traps, German, 152
Bradley, General Omar N.,
    24, 44, 45, 110, 120,
    126, 157
Browning Automatic Rifle,
    102

plan to cross English
Channel, 10, Chapter V
Normandy, France, 29, 43,
44, 51, 54, 60, 73, 75,
76, 85, 95, 98, 101, 133,
147, 151, 154, 161, 168

Omaha Beach, 30, 44, 98,
112–127, 168
Oradour-sur-Glâne, France,
146
Orne River, France, 30, 77,
80, 95, 127
Otway, Lieutenant Colonel
Terence, 80–81
OVERLORD, code name for
the Allied invasion of
Occupied Europe, 10,
23, 24, 29, 37, 39, 44,
45, 46, 47, 50, 51,
53, 54, 56, 58, 60, 63,
66, 70, 73, 91, 93, 101,
120, 136, 146, 154,
166, 170; artificial
seaports, 39–42;
logistics, 39; manpower
buildup, 30–33;
rehearsals for invasion,
64–66; security
precautions, 60–63;
selecting the invasion
site, 27–30; storm delays
invasion, 66–68; tricks
to deceive the enemy,
47–49; weapons buildup,
33–36

Panzer, German tank,
divisions
Twelfth SS, 94, 136, 147,
148; Twenty-first, 136;
Second SS, 146; *Panzer
Lehr,* 94, 136, 148
Paris, France, 164
Pas de Calais, 27, 29, 47, 94
Patch, Lieutenant General
Alexander, 164
Patton, Major General
George S., Jr., 48–49,
161, 162, 163, 164
Pearl Harbor, 4
PLUTO, underwater oil
pipeline, 42
Plymouth, England, 96
Pointe de Hoe, France, 120
poison gas, 102
Port-en-Bessin, France, 129
PT, Patrol Torpedo boat, 96

Queen Elizabeth, 30
Queen Mary, 30

RAF, Royal Air Force, 9,
53, 65–66, 105
Radio Berlin, 22
Ramsay, Admiral Sir
Bertram H., 24
Ranville, France, 82
Resistance, 57–59, 146
Ridgeway, Major General
Matthew B., 86, 90
Rommel, Field Marshal
Erwin, 8–9, 14–15, 17,
18, 20, 22, 23, 24,

29, 44, 85, 92, 113,
135, 139, 160, 164
"Rommel's Asparagus,"
anti-glider traps, 18, 84
Roosevelt, President
Franklin D., 4, 7, 139
Roosevelt, President
Theodore, 109
Roosevelt, Brigadier General
Theodore, Jr., 101–112
Royal Marine, 132
Rudder, Lieutenant
Colonel James F.,
120–121
Rundstedt, Field Marshal
Gerd von, 12–13, 15, 18,
56, 94, 95, 124, 136,
139, 158, 159
Russia, 9–10

Saint-Lô, France, 159, 160
Sainte-Mère-Eglise, France,
86, 88, 90, 95, 106
Schlieben, General von, 157
Second United States Army
Ranger Battalion,
120–121

Seventh United States Army,
164
Sioux Indians, 60
snipers, 152
Southampton, England, 97
Steele, Private John, 88
Summers, Sergeant Harrison,
90–91
Sword Beach, 30, 77, 80, 98,
134, 136, 150

Taylor, Colonel George A.,
128
Taylor, Major General
Maxwell D., 85
Tedder, Air Chief Marshal
Sir Arthur, 24
Third United States Army,
49, 161

"Ultra," secret code machine,
9
Utah Beach, 30, 75, 85,
106–112

warships, Allied, 97; USS
Texas, 97, 125